FACING INTERVIEWS

Om Asatoma Satgamaya
Tamasoma Jyotirgamaya
Mrityorma Amritam Gamaya

Let Us Lead From Untruth To Truth
From Darkness To Light
From Mortality To Immortality.
(1-3-28, *Brihadaranyaka Upanishad*)

Gayatri Mantra
Om Bhur, Bhuvah, Suvah
Tat Savitur Verenayam
Bhargo Devasya Dhimahi
Dhiyo Yo Naa Prachodayat
(*Yajurveda* 36-3)

Om, Who is Dearer than Our Breath
Is Self Subsistent.
All Knowledge and All Bless.
We Meditate upon That Adorable Effulgence of the
Resplendent Vivified of the Macrocosm, Savita,
May He Illumine Our Intellects Unto The Right Path.

FACING INTERVIEWS
Be confident and make an impact

Dr NIRAJ KUMAR
M.Com. (Bus.Admin.), PhD., LlB.,
A.M.S.P.I., F.M.S.P.I., F.A.I.M.C., B.I.A.M, M.D. (AM)
Gold Medallist, National Awardee & Paul Harris Fellow
Advisor: Columbia Holistic University, California, U.S.A.

Former Head & Director
Department of Business Administration
University of Lucknow

STERLING PAPERBACKS
An imprint of
Sterling Publishers (P) Ltd.
A-59, Okhla Industrial Area, Phase-II,
New Delhi-110020.
Tel: 26387070, 26386209; Fax: 91-11-26383788
E-mail: mail@sterlingpublishers.com
ghai@nde.vsnl.net.in
www.sterlingpublishers.com

Facing Interviews
© 2009, Dr Niraj Kumar
ISBN 978 81 207 4780 7
Reprint 2012

All rights are reserved.
No part of this publication may be reproduced, stored in a retrieval system or transmitted, in any form or by any means, mechanical, photocopying, recording or otherwise, without prior written permission of the original publisher.

Printed in India
Printed and Published by Sterling Publishers Pvt. Ltd.,
New Delhi-110 020.

DEDICATION

*Without whose inspiration & blessings
the efforts of the author was impossible
The book is dedicated to Sai Baba of Shirdi with love & respect*

PREFACE

I have attempted to write the present book in a concise form that I had always longed for in the different phases of my life. I have faced many group discussions and interviews and have always felt the need for someone to teach me how to deal with them. I have succeeded in some and failed in some. The most unforgettable one was that, which I faced just after passing out of my post graduation in Business Administration at the age of 22 years in the year 1974; more than three decades ago.

The board comprised of top bureaucrats of the government, top business executives besides world's renowned, and so called "Management Guru's" for a very high profile job in the government sector. Though ultimately I was selected, it is another thing that finally I declined the offer. But this definitely provided me with the expertise to present myself before any board either for group discussions or for interviews.

Thus this book, like any other, has a long ancestry. Many people and experiences have shaped my thinking over the years. In this respect, it is honest and accurate to say that work on this manuscript began a long time ago.

Despite this qualification, what follows is primarily the product of thirty years of direct involvement in thousands of group discussions and interview boards. During this period, I have profited immensely from working with many distinguished thinkers and doers, in both government and the private sector.

I am fortunate to now sit on the other side of the table as a board member for group discussions or interviews, having interviewed over thousands of candidates from graduate students wanting to be admitted into colleges, to management trainees, supervisors and managers at all levels. I have discovered that irrespective of age, education and experience there are certain common fundamental principles that emerged in successful interviews. There were certain factors that made an impact on me as a member of these boards. I find it satisfying to share my experience with those of you who will be appearing for interviews.

An interview is an opportunity to present oneself for selection. Interviews have become an essential and critical part of our lives. This is especially true in our competitive world where selectors have numerous candidates to choose from and an interview becomes the means of differentiating one candidate from the other.

The main idea behind an interview is to determine the personal suitability of the candidate for a particular job. The interview is employed as supplementary to the written examination and is an additional test at which the personal qualities of the candidate such as intelligence, behaviour, ready wit, presence of mind and habits are assessed.

The process of interviews starts very early in one's life. It starts at the age of three or four years when one goes for admission to a nursery school. Most of us remember it as a frightening experience because of the new environment, the new faces and, above all, the separation from the warmth and comfort of our parents' presence. One was forced to face 'aliens' asking strange questions. Our parents may have thought us simple and naive but we were quick to sense their own anxiety, the cries of the other children and the hustle and bustle, which seemed so unnatural. The whole exercise was so strange and confusing that, whether we were conscious of it or not, it laid the seeds of fear of being interviewed. Consequently, interviews became for us a much-dreaded happening.

One had to continue facing interviews as one moved from junior to middle to high school or when one changed schools. The parent-teacher meetings caused us many anxious moments as our progress was discussed and we feared reprisal for negative feedback given by our teacher. The succession of interviews never seemed to end. There were interviews for entering college and later, the critical

Preface

interviews for a job. For many who read this book, the interview process will continue for higher positions in their organisations, transfers, performance appraisals, etc. During the succession of interviews comes the crucial junction— marriage. Irrespective of how the life-partners get together, the interview with the prospective in-laws can be an awkward and sometimes even an embarrassing experience. The list of interviews seems unending — we face it with our banker when we ask for a loan, with the government office when we want pension, social security or a ration card, with the income tax officer for tax returns and refunds and so on.

The candidate must not forget that the interviewers are persons of wide knowledge and experience. They are able to judge the real character and worth of a person by his speech, expressions and self-presentation. In fact, they have a mental picture of the person who would be best fitted for the job and they can judge how far the candidate coincides with this person who is their *Ideal candidate.*

What makes interviews awesome and frightening is the factor of success or failure. We face an interview for something, which is important enough to alter the course of our life. The stakes are often high, making the interview an occasion of' 'life or death'. Failure in an interview is humiliating, shameful and we may even begin to question our self-worth. On the other hand, success brings pride not only to us but to the family, community, neighbourhood and our alma mater.

We would naturally like to, figuratively speaking, put our best foot forward in an interview. What really happens is often the contrary in spite of our best intentions. The pressure of wanting to succeed against seemingly heavy odds often ends in blunders and forgetfulness. Suddenly, the goal that we have been striving for becomes unattractive and fearsome. Our uncertainties and nervousness make us wonder what is going to happen in the interview. We look for somebody or some book that will answer the question that crowd our minds. Coaching schools provide facilities to prepare us for some entrance tests such as GMAT, TOEFL,

MBA, SSB, etc. However, few schools would actually prepare us to deal successfully with an interview.

The candidate, therefore, has to give his best in the group discussions and interviews. He must remember that the first impression is the last impression.

I have chosen not to furnish any footnotes, references, or technical texts to support the concepts or ideas in this book. My purpose was not to produce a scholarly work for the specialist, but to write a practical and readable guide for lay people. The thoughts and examples must make sense on their own. If they don't, even a divine footnote cannot provide salvation.

I have "painted with a broad brush," so you will not become mired in technicality or legalese. This was done to make it easy to understand the broad underlying concepts. It is not my intention to prescribe behaviour or tell you what you should want. Instead, my aim is to illuminate your reality and its opportunities. In doing so, I will point out thought and behaviour that may be limiting you, as well as options and alternatives from which you can choose. Each of you will then, within your own comfort and belief system, have a way of getting what you want, based on your unique needs.

Last but not the least, this presentation would definitely help to train the minds of the readers, so that they could appear more confident in group discussions and interviews and finally emerge with flying colours. It is hoped that it would inculcate the basic principles and values in candidates so that they could appear with confidence and face group discussions and interviews cheerfully, and with all confidence whether they are facing these for competitive examinations or for a job.

I wish all the readers a happy reading and success in your future group discussions and interviews.

C-4/8, River Bank Colony,   **Dr NIRAJ KUMAR**
Lucknow - 226 018

CONTENTS

Preface vii

Prologue 1

1. ESSENTIALS OF AN INTERVIEW 6
   - Interviews in Right Perspective ■ Purpose of an Interview ■ The Interviewer ■ The Interview Room ■ Personal Interview: A. Knowledge, B. Career Plan, C. Communication Skills, D. Analytical and Conceptual Ability, E. Personal Bearing ■ What The Interviewee Has At Stake

2. INTERVIEW PREPARATION 21
   - Preparation For The Interview ■ Your Attitude Matters ■ Negative Attitudes: The Opportunist Attitude, The Depressive Attitude, The Angry Attitude, The Desperate Attitude, The Half-Hearted Attitude, The Emotionally Unstable Attitude, The Know-It-All Attitude, The Irrational Attitude, The Sloppy Attitude, The Non-Conformist Attitude ■ Positive Attitudes: A Visionary Attitude, A Positive Attitude Helps, A Realistic Attitude ■ Self-Appraisal ■ Overcome Fears ■ Interview Or Job

3. ASSESS YOURSELF BEFORE AN INTERVIEW 36
   - How To Assess Yourself ■ Common Worries ■ Calm Your Nerves ■ Have Faith In Your CV ■ Focus On Others ■ Be Aware Of Environment ■ Forget The Significance Of The Interview ■ Tell Yourself You'll Enjoy ■ Rehearse ■ Some Guiding Factors: Know Yourself, Good Knowledge, Reasoning, Don't Be Prejudiced, The Right Attitude, Confidence, Honesty Is The Best Policy, Think Before You Speak, Personality, Speaking Manners, Be A Good Listener, Etiquettes, Expression, Alertness, Manners, Smartness, Dress, ■ Preparation Stage: Practice Makes A Man Perfect

4. PROBABLE QUESTIONS 67
   - Anticipating Questions: Describe Yourself, What Your Last Boss Was Like? How You Fit The Job? Where You Want To Be 10 Years From Now? What Your Ideal Boss Would Be Like? ■ Questions On Inconsistencies ■ Any Questions ■ Some Tips

5. THE RIGHT APPROACH 74
■ A Psychological Approach ■ Your Body Language ■ The Wrong Approach ■ Some Suggested Questions For Academic Interviews: Questions to Test Your Knowledge or Habits, Questions to Test Your Personality and Attitudes, Questions to Test Your Social Awareness

6. PRE-INTERVIEW GUIDELINES 89
■ Final Pre-Interview Checklist ■ Useful Hints For The Candidate ■ Not To Forget: Study The Copy Of Your Resume, Try To "Lead" The Interviewer, Be Your Natural Self, Exaggeration, Bluffing And Boastfulness, Listen More Talk Less ■ Some Do's And Don'ts: Do's, Don'ts

7. SAMPLE INTERVIEWS 98
■ Mock Interview No. 1: The Candidate ■ Mock Interview No. 2: The Candidate

8. A FINAL WORD 125
■ A Final Word ■ Interview—A Table Tennis Game ■ Preparation ■ Change Your Mindset ■ Forget Fear Of Interview For A Job ■ Forget Fear Of Rejection ■ Calming Techniques ■ Preparation Before The Interview : 1. Before The Interviews, 2. Sample Questions, 3. Organisation's Expectations, 4. Pick Your Outfit And Go To Bed Early ■ The Day Of The Interview ■ At The Interview ■ While Giving Answers To Questions ■ Winning Interview Technique: 1. Dress Appropriately, 2. Be Punctual, 3. Body Language Says A Lot, 4. Answer Truthfully, 5. Keep Your Cool ■ Some Unusual Hints

9. AFTER THE INTERVIEW 139
■ After The Interview ■ Some Probable Questions And Answers: *Why Is The Question Asked?* ■ Some Ready To Use Checklists: Carrying Your Documents And Testimonials ■ Points To Ponder: Style Of Interviewer, Shaking The Hand Of The Interviewer, Play The Interview In Your Mind Before The Actual Interview, Mock Interviews Can Be A Great Help, Questions Related To Your Subject, Maintain Eye Contact, Importance Of Quoting Examples, Turning Failure Into Success, Relax Before The Interview, Day Dreaming, Deep Breathing, Warm Your Face

Epilogue   179

PROLOGUE

Reaching the stage of interview or group discussion is by itself an indication that you have already cleared many a hurdle on the way to your success in getting the desired admission or a job appointment. The stage of group discussion and interview is the final stage before being selected for a professional course or getting appointed to a job. There are some companies where the group discussion is succeeded by an interview too, particularly in those, which summon aspirants directly without taking a written examination.

Interviews are nothing to be afraid of. These are the means for the employer to know whether you are fit for the job or not. Think from a personal point of view. If you go to a shop, you would certainly ask the shopkeeper, why you should buy this product and why not from a competitor. In whether a group discussion or an interview, the same thing applies. The organisation is trying to know why it should hire you and not others.

In other words, an interview is a means to sell oneself to the employer. Appearing at this crucial stage needs due preparation. And we shall try our best to help you out.

So you feel that you are ready to hit the job market, congratulations! Now you would like to prepare yourself for success in interviews and group discussions. The very fact that you are reading this shows that you are willing to learn and have understood that there is a need to prepare yourself You recognise the fact that if you handle this important step of your life well it will have a long-term impact on your life. It is beautifully said that *'the journey of a thousand miles must begin with a single step'*. So the group discussion and interview may be the first small step in a journey of your working career, which will go on for a long time.

There exists a great possibility that you may have just come out of college and might be carrying a lot of habits from student life. You must also be having many preconceived notions about professional life. Alternatively, you could be a person already gainfully employed and now you are looking for a better or different job. In case you are already employed and are looking for a change, your interview will largely depend on the reason for seeking the change.

Let us face interviews confidently. Confident candidates perform well at group discussions and interviews. They project a good image of themselves and their abilities and they make it their business to do their homework beforehand. They research the company and gain interview practice. In short, they sell themselves, but more importantly they inspire the employer's confidence in them. Thus, confident interviewees are the successful ones. For they give the employer more reason to say 'yes' to choosing them than to say 'no'. Hence, it is in your interest to develop the same degree of self-confidence. This book will show you how to do this. The good news is that it is not as difficult as you might think!

Self-confidence is rooted in experience, knowledge and practice. If you lack confidence or have had yours knocked by circumstances, don't despair because, given the time and patience, it can be rebuilt.

For the vast majority of us, getting an interview call, or making sure that a job opportunity does not slip away, can be an all-consuming obsession in our lives at some time or the other. Our palms perspire, our throats run dry and our temples throb as the days go by and the pressure builds up!

As a result of this tension, when fickle opportunity does finally knock on our door, we are unprepared. Therefore, we are unable to give it our best shot. This is a great tragedy indeed!

Prologue

It need not be so at all. Each one of us has knowledge, skills, aptitude, potential, ability and a burning desire to succeed. What we do not always have is the training and guidance to bring our qualities to the forefront, to package ourselves attractively and to make ourselves desirable in the eyes of the potential employer.

On the one hand, we need to acquire thorough and dispassionate knowledge about ourselves, our personal strengths and weaknesses. On the other hand, we need an understanding of the job's requirements. Then, we need the skill to match our strengths with the job requirements and offer the package to the potential employer with a degree of salesmanship that rarely comes naturally to us.

Sounds like an impossible task? Not at all! These are skills you can learn. What you need is commitment, perseverance and above all, *good guidance*. The very fact that you have picked up this book is a measure of your commitment and your willingness to work hard. What remains is good guidance.

However, to build your confidence remember the following:

Do more than Exist,	LIVE
Do more than Touch,	FEEL
Do more than Look,	OBSERVE
Do more than Read,	ABSORB
Do more than Hear	LISTEN
Do more than Listen	THINK
Do more than Think,	UNDERSTAND
Do more than Talk,	SAY SOMETHING

"SAY NA"
I Love You
But you should not forget:
Child's Attitude
Teenager's Dream
Adult's Desire

Old people's Memories
Believe in Life
Therefore, Believe in your Dreams
However the crux is:
It is Nice to be
Important
BUT
It is MORE IMPORTANT

To be NICE

However, one should always remember:
The FORMULA TO SUCCESS IS:

A small truth to make our life 100% successful!!!

A	B	C	D	E	F	G	H	I	J	K	L	M
1	2	3	4	5	6	7	8	9	10	11	12	13
N	O	P	Q	R	S	T	U	V	W	X	Y	Z
14	15	16	17	18	19	20	21	22	23	24	25	26

THUS: HARDWORK = 8+1+18+4+23+15+18+11= 98%
LOVE = 12+15+22+5 = 54%
BUT
None of them Makes 100%!!!
Is it MONEY? ... NO,
Since MONEY = (13+15+14+5+25 = 72% Only)
Is it LEADERSHIP? ... NO,
Since LEADERSHIP = (12+5+1+4+5+18+19+8+9+16 = 97%) Only
But Do not worry!!!

Every Problem has a solution
Only if we perhaps change ours
ATTITUDE
It is our **'ATTITUDE'** towards life that makes us **'SUCCESSFUL'**
SEE YOURSELF
'ATTITUDE' = 1+20+20+9+20+21+4+5 = 100%
AND
Above all
HONESTY = (9+15+14+5+19+20+25) = 106%
So, be honest since it is more scoring than your attitude.

Now stop getting worried, nervous or scared of group discussions and interviews. Just follow the techniques given in the following pages and GET SET GO!

1

ESSENTIALS OF AN INTERVIEW

Interviews in Right Perspective

At the outset you would do well to get rid of certain wrong notions, and along with them, of certain fears about the essential selection ritual called Interview. First, as many candidates fear (some spend a few sleepless nights worrying about it) an interview is not a cross-examination where you are subjected to a barrage of merciless questioning by a committee of superior beings bent on exposing your ignorance.

The Oxford Dictionary defines an interview as 'a face-to-face meeting, especially for the purpose of obtaining a statement or for assessing the qualities of a candidate'. 'Interview' is derived from the French word 'entrevoir' which means 'glimpse'. This, therefore, indicates a physical meeting of people with two possible objectives:

(a) *To obtain a statement or opinion* – as is done when film stars are interviewed to get their views on any particular role, or when the prime minister is interviewed to get a statement on the result of his discussion with another political leader.

(b) *To assess a person for selection* – such as interviews for jobs, admission to educational institutions or even for finding a suitable partner in marriage.

We will be concerned with the second objective with special reference to interviews for jobs and admission to educational institutions. The principles governing an interview would, however, remain the same even for interviews having the first objective.

Interview means the meeting of two or more people for a specific purpose. Earlier, the purpose of interviews used to be to find a suitable employee for the job, but today its application is wide. Besides selecting prospective employees, this technique is also adopted for selection of students for various courses, etc. Even otherwise, the application of interview is found in almost all aspects of life – electorate interviews prospective legislators; customers' interview shopkeepers while selecting a product; and so on.

An interview is not a question-answer session. Nor are the people who interview you basically very different from what you are. Only, they have more of a general experience of life and some of them are adept at the art of identifying people who would prove to be the fit candidates for the purpose for which they have been selecting.

The members of the selection committee are provided with the summary of your biodata, your scholastic achievements, and your score at the written test and your performance at the group discussions. You can expect them to treat you with consideration; your name has appeared on the merit list – not an ultimate achievement on your part, they know. They are eager to see you to confirm, once and for all, in a face-to-face situation, whether in fact, you are among the suitable persons they are looking for.

The objective of the interview board is to ascertain your mental alertness, your general knowledge, the breadth of your outlook, and to obtain an impression of your personality. You know, of course, that your personality is not only your appearance, but also the complex part of your feelings, emotions, opinions, attitudes, your drives and ambitions representing your unique adjustment to your environment. In the short time that is available to them, the interviewers wish to gather an impression of you as a person.

Purpose of an Interview

It seems clear from the definition and objectives given above that the purpose of an interview is to create an opportunity for people to meet and converse with each other on a matter of mutual benefit. The participants include an interviewer or interviewers who pose questions relating to the objective of the interview and an interviewee who answers them. This does not exclude the interviewee from asking questions too and therein lies the concept of *mutuality* where both parties benefit. A successful interview cannot be a one-way street. It must be an occasion for discussion in which questions and answers are posed by both sides. Most of us fear being interviewed because we approach the interview as a *one-sided affair*.

An interview provides an opportunity to make possible a two-way communication between two parties, one of whom is selling his organisation, and the other selling himself. Thus, an interview is a mutual exchange of ideas, information and impressions. However, it remains a truth that in this two-way communication, the interviewer or the employer has a better stand. But it should not sound pessimistic. The interviewer is undertaking this exercise to find out a person who would fit his job well and help the organisation grow and progress. It makes it explicit that the interviewer is not there to reject people, but to select people, who, according to his view point, should be there.

Thus, an interview is an exercise also where an interviewee tries to sell himself. Keeping this in view, an interviewee needs to prepare himself for this *important occasion*, in true sense of the word so that no misconceptions, misunderstandings, and ambiguities arise; but conversely, the interviewee is selected for the job on the basis of his presentation of himself in the best way he could, so that he may appear to be the best *choice* available.

The main idea behind an interview is to determine the personal suitability of the candidate for a particular job. It

Essentials of an Interview

is the final hurdle, which the candidate has to cross in order to get the job that he seeks. The interview is employed as supplementary to the written examination and is an additional test at which the personal qualities of the candidate such as intelligence, behaviour, ready wit, presence of mind and habits are assessed. A candidate may have obtained a first class degree but he may not fare well at the interview and may be found unfit for the job for which he has applied. Many candidates who pass the written test with credit are unable to impress the interviewers and are, therefore, rejected.

Interview is an important stage before final selection is made for any post. Only a few posts are filled without interview. Generally for each post seven to eight candidates are called for interview. There are certain posts where interview alone plays the decisive role. Therefore any one seeking a job must prepare himself for the interview to avoid frustration.

The candidate has to remember that the interviewers are persons of wide knowledge and experience. They are able to judge the real character and worth of a person by his speech, expressions and self-presentation. They know everything about the job and the type of work and responsibilities that the candidate has to shoulder. They have a mental picture of the person who would be best fitted for the job and they can judge how far the candidate coincides with this person who is their ideal. The interviewers would not mind if the candidate is a little short of their expectations but he has to prove that he has a real aptitude for the job and can acquit himself creditably in it.

The candidate, therefore, has to give his best to the interviewers. He must remember that the first impression is the last impression. In the very beginning he should impress the interviewer with his knowledge, intelligence and confidence. He should so manipulate the questioning or the trend of conversation that it may project his good points and hide his weaknesses. The candidate should not get perturbed when the interviewer tries to screen him and play on his nerves. He should try to retain his politeness, cheerfulness and patience to the end displaying his interest and sincerity in the interview all the time. The candidate should never feel offended or annoyed at questions of personal type which he would otherwise not have liked to be asked but should answer them sincerely and in a pleasing and convincing way avoiding false or overstatements. Brief, to the point, but clear expression is always likely to impress the members of the interview board.

The Interviewer

It is worthwhile for the candidate to know something about the interviewer. The first thing, that the candidate should know, is that generally the interviewer is a highly placed person have an abundant fund of experience at his command. The interview board consists of high government officials drawn from different departments. The main aim of the interviewer is not to test the candidate's knowledge of any particular subject. That is tested by means of written papers. His main aim is to test his mental alertness, his presence of mind, his general knowledge, his capacity to grapple with problems, his intelligence, his outlook towards life and to get a complete impression of his personality.

Interviewers for different types of services have different aims in mind. The aim of the interviewer, who happens to be the employer also, is quite different from that of the interviewers who have to select a candidate for a government post. While the employer would search for a special or particular quality in the candidate, the board of interviewers would give importance to the personal and general qualities of the candidate, as the candidate when appointed may have to work in different departments, at different places and in different situations. In such a case, qualities like adaptability and general intelligence are more important than the

Essentials of an Interview

candidate's knowledge of a particular subject. In a business concern or a private establishment the employee has to work according to the directions of the proprietor or the directors. The government official, on the other hand, has very often to take vital decisions all by him. Therefore, a candidate for a high government post must possess more than average intelligence, acumen and capacity of taking decisions and should possess wide interests apart from his educational achievements. We have, therefore, to make a distinction between the interview boards for a private job and the interview boards for government jobs.

Whether the interview is for a private job or for a government service, the candidate must remember that he has to appear before men of wide experience and knowledge, and that higher the post, higher will be the stature of the interviewers. Sometimes, they may be giants before whom the knowledge and experience of the candidate may pale into insignificance. To face them, is a challenge to meet, for which, a candidate has to be very well prepared. He must pay proper respect and regard to the dignity and status of the interviewer. The candidate should not be misled by their apparently simple looking clothes and looks, small talks and jokes.

Knowledge about the type of the interviewer can be very helpful for the candidate in adapting himself to them. After knowing the interviewer the candidate can fit himself to his particular demand and tendencies. The candidate should be able to judge the interviewer as soon as he starts throwing questions. He should not make the least delay in answering the questions of the interviewer. He should be able to interpret the questions of the interviewer correctly and answer them as correctly as possible. The interviewer should get the impression that the candidate is attentive towards him and he is taking keen interest in his questions. Even apparently, silly questions from the interviewer should be dealt with all sincerity and seriousness by the candidate. Answer all the questions clearly and convincingly. While it is imperative to be quick in making the reply, hastiness of an awkward type must be avoided. Listen to the question of the interviewer patiently, understand it confidently and then alone put across your reply in a clear and convincing way stressing upon things in a natural manner, if any emphasis, on a particular point is required by the situation. You should behave most naturally and normally and there should be no sign of nervousness on your face or in your speech. Even if you commit some mistakes in answering questions, you can win the favour and liking of the interviewers by showing your attention and respect to them.

There is no reason why the candidate should be afraid of the interviewers as they are also normal human beings and their main job is to discover the true personality of the candidate and find out his latent qualities. The interviewer is there not to baffle you with unnecessary questions and to reject you but to select you provided you possess the minimum of qualities required for the job. So be open and sincere to the interviewer so that he may judge you correctly and discover your hidden qualities.

The interviewer is looking at you as the person who would best fit the job not only in accordance with the skills and/or specialisation you are being selected for, but also for your personal traits as an entire person who can interact with other people in the organisation and persons concerned with the organisation.

Interviewers also understand that an interviewee may not be himself due to a number of reasons like depressions, ambitions, over confidence, stress, atmosphere, etc. Therefore, interviewers generally encourage interviewees to be their own selves, so that proper personal attributes may be made out. So, don't be afraid of interviews. Be honest, thoughtful and frank. Your endeavours should be to project 'the real you'.

An interview is the basis on which the structure of the edifice of mutual interaction and sound human reaction is based in the period after having secured employment and placement.

The Interview Room

It would be helpful for the candidate if he has a mental picture of the interview room. In the middle of the room, facing the exit, there is a big table. Seated in the centre is the chairman of the interview board with a few members on his right and a few on the left. There is a chair for the candidate on the other side of the table just opposite the chairman, etc.

Personal Interview

Explicitly or implicitly, the conversation at the interview that is conducted for educational institutes for higher learning and companies that are looking for young graduates to recruit will be directed towards probing into the following traits of your personality.

A. Knowledge

- Knowledge of current affairs (economic, social and political problems facing management in India)
- Depth and breadth in the area of specilisation in studies, or your job if you are holding one
- Awareness of social problems (poverty, inequality, justice, population, food, housing health, etc.)

A person who is ignorant of his surroundings is a liability. Though it is not possible to know everything, one is expected to have a broad idea of the happenings in the social, political and economic fields. You will not be expected to know these matters in all their details. What you will be expected to know, however, are the main facts, events and trends such as, those appearing in the daily newspapers. If you wish to get acquainted with current affairs, there is no substitute for reading the daily newspaper; at least 60 of them preceding your interview. It is also a good habit to preserve clippings of important news items.

Next, the subjects you studied. These often help the interviewer to start a conversation with you. "What was your favourite subject at the college level?" is a familiar question. If your answer is, "economics," be prepared for the next question, which will most likely be on that subject. The intent will be to probe the depth and breadth of your interest in what you profess to be your favourite subject. If you cannot explain the superiority of indifference curve analysis over the traditional demand and supply approach or if you have not heard of Adam Smith, Karl Marx, or of the General Theory, The Affluent Society or the Asian Drama, or Paul Samuelson, Milton Friedman or John Kenneth Galbraith, your knowledge of Economics has been superficial indeed.

B. Career Plan

- Whether you have a definite career plan or you are the sorts who applies pointlessly to every course advertised in newspapers
- Whether your goals regarding career are clear-cut and if you are determined to pursue them seriously
- Whether your goals reflect, besides self-interest, high (not romantic) ideals, altruism, generosity and a sense of moral values

To have clear vocational goals is a sign of maturity. If you are clear regarding your career, you will not falter while answering the question, "Why do you wish to seek a career in Management?" Or, if it is a girl, "Suppose you get married, would you still continue your career, as a Manager?" If you have, made up your mind on a career for yourself and have planned carefully to pursue it assiduously, you would have already answered such questions convincingly to yourselves.

The goals, people set for themselves also reflect their inner drives and ambitions. What is it you want most out of life? Money? Yes? No? Be honest to yourself. (Money isn't

Essentials of an Interview

everything of course. But you would be wise to earn a good lot of it before talking such nonsense). Whether you term it as having a "comfortable life" or a "decent standard of living," you need money. That is about one of the honest goals most people work for most of the time and you are probably not an exception.

However, a manager's job is not the one for those who wish to make 'pots and pots' of money and for some reason – 'roll in it', as the trite phrases go. The job offers you a good financial security but many managers would tell you that it is only one aspect and not a very important one, after a time at least – of the pains and pleasures of a manager's job. Among the highly prized opportunities it offers is challenge; an opportunity to lead groups of people to purposeful activity and an opportunity to be creative (not in the artistic sense), but in the humbler sense of being useful to the people around and to the community at large. This last one, we shall term (for the want of a better word) as 'idealism', which in this context simply means a sense of duty towards the society and an innate desire to make one's surroundings better than one found them.

Excess idealism is as disagreeable as a complete lack of it. A Don Quixote is ridiculous, but so is the lack luster existence of a self-bound egoist.

C. Communication Skills

- Is the candidate sure and unhesitant?
- Is he clear and distinct?
- Is he articulate and persuasive?

It is a pleasure to listen to a person who can convey what he thinks in a clear manner and in a clearly audible voice. The manner you speak, your choice of words, intonation and your accent are important and will be definitely marked by those whom you *are* facing. Clear communication also means clear thinking. Avoid expressing vague opinions or risking descriptions of things you are not sure about. Finally, communication ability also means an ability to listen attentively. Those who lack listening ability frequently have to "Beg your pardon, Sir". Worse still, their answers often have no relevance to the questions asked by the interviewer, with the result that the interviewer is forced to repeat his questions with a mild remonstration, "Listen to my question, first; I asked you..." One, who communicates effectively, first listens attentively and then after a pause for a couple of seconds, answers the question in a calm tone of voice.

D. Analytical And Conceptual Ability

- Is the candidate logical and analytical?
- Does he synthesise his experiences and reading?
- Can he apply abstract concepts or principles to concrete real life situations?

"Do you agree that India is an industrial society?" The apparently well read candidate replies somewhat as follows: "About 70 per cent of the Indians are dependent on agriculture or agriculture-based industries. However, recent statistics shows that investment in industries as well as industrial production has also been increasing. Therefore, it would be right to say that India is a progressing, as well as a growing industrialised nation. The answer doesn't lack information. What it lacks, however, is a capacity to synthesise the information and the ability to arrive at a logical and cogent conclusion.

Many are good at seeing isolated things, but lack the capacity to synthesise their observation. Many see individual stars, but few the constellations. The capacity to synthesise or to relate in a meaningful whole, the facts one observes or reads is a high-rated quality in anyone who wishes to be a man of action. So is the capacity to apply abstract and theoretical concepts to practical situations.

Progress, many a time comes in the guise of an idea, a concept or a theory. Most of the so called learned have read and digested all the hair-splitting details about these ideas.

Essentials of an Interview

But the practical man who has to profit from these has to go a couple of steps ahead. He has to cultivate both, insight and skill to tell the feasible from the non-feasible and has to apply the feasible ones to day-to-day situations, which means he cannot merely let it remain a theory in the books but has to be aware of the relevance of the concepts to everyday life.

E. Personal Bearing

- Is the candidate composed, collected and confident? Or is he nervous, shy and fidgety?
- Does he show a liking for hard work? Or has he a marked preference for taking to easy ways?
- Does he show initiative and self-discipline? Is he a bookworm or is he a person with many sides to him?

The general manner of a self-confident individual reflects poise and has a certain impact on the people whom he is facing. He looks people straight in their eyes in a quiet friendly manner. (Selectors complain that they are often horrified by the looks the candidates give them). His confidence is the result of a realistic appraisal of his abilities and he has sufficient confidence in his assets and a clear awareness of his shortcomings.

He avoids direct, blunt or curt remarks. He owns up his mistakes or ignorance without feeling terribly embarrassed about it. His manner suggests that it's bad he doesn't know the answer, but after all it isn't possible to know answers to all the questions.

It is definitely a mark of self-discipline if, in your college years, you were diligent to those subjects you disliked. It shows lack of self-discipline if you were not able to make yourself 'dig deeply enough' to master the subject. You can hardly claim to be disciplined if you give an impression of being conditioned by a comfortable, soft and easy life.

A person with initiative is a self-starter and does not wait to be told what to do. He tries to reach out for ever-increasing responsibilities. He demonstrates willingness to depart from the status quo in order to accomplish a given task in a new and perhaps more efficient manner.

Next, for undergoing a tough professional course or to undertake a difficult assignment a person who is conditioned to work hard for long durations is preferred. If you seem phlegmatic, reflecting a possible below average energy level, they would be justified in your own interest in not selecting you.

Perseverance is the ability to continue with whatever you have undertaken to do until it is completed, resisting any tendency to become distracted. People who hop from one job to another and students, who opt for too many courses without completing any successfully, are a bad risk. People, who are consistent and show high personal standards of workmanship, naturally command more respect.

Finally, your hobbies and extra-curricular activities are many a time, pointers to a person's real interests and preoccupations. It is dismal to hear a candidate saying he has no hobbies. It indicates a dull, colourless existence of a workhorse who is not interested in anything beyond the narrow world of routine or his textbooks. Those of you who have too many hobbies, however, would do well to mention a few of them (one or two), which you think are really worth mentioning and which are truly your hobbies.

Well, these are some of your personality traits that the selectors could be interested to find out. It can be assumed that most of those who make the grade and appear on the merit list have these desirable traits to a certain extent. So, be confident and prepare yourself to answer all the questions convincingly and which you expect them to ask. Some of the questions will be general in nature, but most of them are likely to be on your personal situation, your preference and your goals and ambitions. Following is a list of some suggested questions. If you can answer these convincingly to yourself, there is a good chance of your repeating the performance at your interview.

What The Interviewee Has At Stake

The greatest stake that an interviewee has is to be selected in the hope of augmenting life's experiences, achieving status and a better quality of life. Interviews are given in order to achieve something better than what one presently has. Hence, one goes for an interview for a better job, higher education or anything else that will take one a step higher on the ladder of success.

Another stake an interviewee has is his own ego. Success in an interview brings about a feeling of self-worth and therefore, a sense of well-being. A boost to one's self-confidence is accompanied with a desire to compete further. Often one's success in an interview becomes a matter of pride for the family, community, school, college, etc. I have often heard staff and students of colleges proudly boasting of their senior students being selected in the foreign services, administrative services, medical colleges or a good company. There is a degree of pride and honour associated with certain interviews.

We have, thus, seen that all those concerned in an interview process have a stake in it. Therefore, it seems apparent that the best way to make an interview truly successful is to take a stance of mutuality where all participants – the organisation, the interviewer and the interviewee attempt to satisfy their respective needs. I recommend a partnership approach where the mood is one of 'give and take'. In a partnership, each member has rights, which need to be respected and honoured. If both approach the interview with equal rights, it can be converted into a very rewarding and mature experience. In most interviews, organisations and interviewers fulfil their rights by getting all the relevant information about an interviewee. You have the right to get all the information you want about the organisation in order to determine whether your decision to join the organisation is a right one or not. Many people claim that jobs are few and hard to come by and in the process forfeit their rights of mutuality. The spirit of the interview is really the state of your mind. If your attitude is to exercise your rights then the tone of the interview becomes one of mutuality, less awesome and more successful.

I recall a candidate who exercised his rights and walked out withdrawing his candidature for further consideration. While getting additional facts from me about the job content, working hours and so on, he discovered that the job profile was not what he had imagined it to be. It did not suit his priorities, temperament and nature and he therefore, withdrew his candidature. Many of us later find to our discomfort, that we had joined organisations and jobs that really did not fit in with our aptitude, temperament and values. Our eagerness to 'get the job' led us to withhold our rights during the interview and thereby join a wrong job.

I am sure you would like to know the kind of questions you can ask of the interviewers. Strictly speaking, there is no limitation to the questions you can ask an interviewer, as long as they are restricted to those concerning the job. Some of the queries that can be posed are the nature of the job content, working hours, salary and benefits, reporting relationships, career growth, the organisation's growth plans, etc. You have a right to know these things and it is this that brings about the mutuality in an interview.

The process of questioning an interviewer must be done with utmost respect and sincerity. Many candidates who approach this task of asking questions do so with arrogance and a brash air of challenge. Such candidates are not selected. Even in those cases where the intention is one of mutuality, the manner in which it is put across is all wrong. Enquiries put to the interviewers, if done with politeness and dignity, help in softening the mood of the interview, however intimidating it might be. A successful interview is, thus, based on a sense of mutuality between the interviewer and the interviewee.

Remember, that an interview where interviewees ask questions is appreciated by the interviewer.

2

INTERVIEW PREPARATION

Preparation For The Interview

Careful preparation is the route to a successful interview. Preparation avoids being taken by surprise and prevents giving away information that it would have been better to keep to yourself. There is more to consider than working out the odd question to ask. For once, at the interview the whole person is in view; and the interviewer would most likely, want to explore certain subjects to probe into and dig deep. Preparation enables you to be open and honest and to feel comfortable with what is being asked and how you are replying. Remember that no amount of preparation will ensure that you get the job, but it will ensure that your performance is your best one.

A candidate has to prepare for the interview, which he is going to face. He has to keep in mind the type of interview that he has to face. He may have to appear before an employer or a board of interviewers. Whatever be the type of interview, the candidate must possess certain general qualities like cheerfulness, politeness, affability, good manners and behaviour. In order to be successful in life it is very necessary that parents and teachers should discover the most suitable career for the child and the child should be made conscious of the responsibilities and possibilities of such a career. His preparations should be directed from the very beginning to fulfil the mission of his life.

As soon as the boy knows what career he has to enter, he has to start preparing for making himself fit for that position in everyway. He should develop qualities, habits and behaviour required for his future call. The future doctor has to cultivate in himself a deep interest in human physiology, biology and chemistry. The future teacher has to develop interest in child psychology, the quality of leadership and individual confidence and so on.

A boy, who thus starts his preparations, will not find the interview either taxing or terrifying. His interest in his career would have led him to gather all the knowledge and information connected with his future job that will give him the confidence without which success at the interview is very doubtful. Such a candidate may fail to answer some questions correctly but he will surely impress the interviewers with his deep interest and liking for the job and will, therefore, win their favour. It is therefore, in the best interest of a boy to start preparations for his future job as early in his life as possible.

You may start preparations with a definite job in mind and even if you never get such a job, nothing is lost. It is certainly a tragedy that you do not get a job which you aspire for but it would certainly be a greater tragedy if you miss the opportunity of getting it simply because you were not prepared for it. You must remember the famous saying that *'opportunity is bald-headed on the back side'*. Therefore, you must be prepared to avail the opportunity as and when it comes to you. There is no shortcut to success. You cannot thumb your way down the highway of life and arrive at any worthwhile destination. All your mental and intellectual resources should be mobilised to face the battle of an interview with a measure of success.

Your Attitude Matters

Before considering how to prepare for the interview, consider first the concept of attitude and your attitude. Are you aware of your attitude during an interview? What unspoken message are you conveying to the prospective employer? I had a client that came for an interview practice who felt that he needed some tips on how to be more assertive in the interview situation. "Assertive?" I asked. He then explained how he had been promised a directorship at work, but after a row with the chairman it had been offered to someone else. So, he was now looking for a better job elsewhere. I said to him that he seemed angry. "Angry," he said. "I'm furious, it is disgusting, I am so mad about what has happened!" He was furious; he spoke quickly and curtly, his lip was tight and he stared hard. It was a difficult task to advise him that his anger was being taken into all interviews that he was attending and that if he wanted to increase his success rate and ease the pressure of his current role, he had to work upon dissolving his anger.

Attitude is crucial to your performance. It is reflected in the tone of your CV and also in the interview. In fact, attitude speaks even louder than what you actually say. This is where most interviewees' trip, as they fail to realise the importance and significance of their attitude, the very thing that may be putting the employer off in choosing them. Attitude is reflected by the choice of vocabulary, facial expressions, behaviour and one's sense of dressing. The true test of attitude is to see it in action. Have a look in the mirror or video a dummy interview. Is this the real you? Do you like what you see? On paper you may have got it right, but at an interview your facial expressions, tone, posture and movements can either confirm or conflict with what you are saying. Is your attitude making others feel warm towards you or withdraw from you?

To make things clearer, listed below are the types of attitudes or states of mind that put employers off. Employers are not looking for a perfect candidate because there is no such thing (although it has been said that imperfect people always want to hire perfect people). However, they are looking for a stable, realistic, positive, visionary candidate who wants a long-term future, a candidate that gives the employer more reason to say 'yes' to him/her than 'no', a candidate that will add value to the company and not one that brings all his or her baggage and problems with him or her. The interviewer may have enough problems of his or her own.

However, if you do recognise yourself as adopting any of the negative attitudes listed below, then it is time for you to change. The secret to your future success is that you are now aware of the importance of attitude and if you do find yourself slipping into this type of behaviour at an interview you can amend it and do so quickly. The message is – if you are in the right frame of mind employers will be more attracted towards you. They will then want you in their team.

Negative Attitudes

The Opportunist Attitude

The opportunist person has no real commitment to an employer and is liable to move on when his or her mood or requirements change. It can be detected when the interviewee gives flippant replies to questions and does not talk about long-term aspirations and desires, partly because the person is unsure of what he or she is. Do you have an opportunist attitude? Do you get bored easily? Do you browse through magazines and papers and only apply for jobs as and when you see something that excites you? Is it the money, car, increased responsibility or opportunities that are attracting you to apply? Action: You need to sort out what you want from your career in the long and short-term.

The Depressive Attitude

A depressive person doesn't want to take responsibility for his or her career. It can be detected by the employer because the candidate blames the company and environment for what has or has not happened. Employers will not be attracted to this person because he or she will need a lot of hand-holding and reassurance, plus he or she will affect the morale of the team.

Do you have a depressive attitude? Do you look for a new job when you are fed up with the one you are currently doing? Do you apply when things get on top of you at work, when you feel that you can't cope and need to escape from the monotony of your current situation? Action: You need to start taking charge of your career, sort out what you want and realise that you can influence your situation. Think about what you enjoy doing, what motivates you and present the good at the interview rather than the bad.

The Angry Attitude

The angry person doesn't win over the employer's approval or support. The angry person talks in terms of how the previous company should have rewarded him. A position is unlikely to be offered as his or her demands and expectations come across as being too high and volatile. Business is about fulfilling value and need and a prospective employer would question whether or not the person has exaggerated the case or has misinterpreted the previous company's promise of reward. The employer would be uneasy about employing this person in case it happened again.

Do you have an angry attitude? Do you start looking for jobs when you feel that you are being overlooked at work? When you notice that your colleagues and subordinates are being promoted and you are not, even though you think you should be? When you don't get the credit for a project you deserve? Or when you feel that your career is not moving as fast as it should be? Action: If you feel you have been unfairly treated or mistreated, beware. Talk to your boss and sort it out. You don't want to carry this disappointment with you for the rest of your career as it could grow with time. At an interview, if the case comes up, it is much better to talk about personality clashes rather than in terms of what you ought to or should have gained. Anyone can have a personality clash and thus it is acceptable.

The Desperate Attitude

Employers are proud of their company or business and want to employ people who hold similar values. Desperate interviewees are those people that see their own needs and situation as far more important than those of the employer.

Do you have a desperate attitude? Are you short of money and out of work? Are you threatened with redundancy? Are you unsure of what you want to do but willing to give any job a try? Action: You must try and see the employer's point of view as well as your own. You may find that a temporary job may ease the financial burden and pressures. You must stress your positive attributes and skills rather than saying that you will do anything, as this is too weak and feeble.

The Half-Hearted Attitude

Half-hearted people give themselves away because they lack stability, conviction and stamina. Employers get the impression that everything is too much effort and that they just can't be bothered. This person often refers to his or her feelings, feelings of guilt, shame and disappointment. Employers will not be attracted to this person because he or she cannot be relied upon to be self-sufficient.

Do you have a half-hearted attitude? Are you easily disappointed and take knocks too personally? Do you need time to heal and lick your wounds after you have been rejected? Do you give up at the first hurdle? Or do you see it

Interview Preparation 27

as a learning process and find out the reasons you weren't selected and work on the tips you have been given? Does your job hunt lose momentum, and then you spend time feeling guilty that nothing is happening on the job front? Action: Work out why you are giving up. Do you really want this job?

The Emotionally Unstable Attitude

Employers want assurances that you will and can do the job. An employer would be concerned if you have suffered any personal or emotional problems that could affect your work performance. Do you have an emotionally unstable attitude? Perhaps you have just experienced bereavement or been through a messy divorce. If divorced or separated, explain briefly the circumstances if these add to your case. Action: If asked about the event, don't fall into the trap of giving the employer all the details. He or she is not interested in this but that you have sorted yourself out. An employer doesn't want to employ all your problems as well, as he or she has enough of his or her own.

The Know-It-All Attitude

A 'know-it-all' person doesn't let others appreciate his or her way of thinking. He or she is so wrapped up in his or her own self-importance and how brilliantly he or she has performed in the past that his or her attitude invites others to put him or her down or see fault in him or her. Of course, employers are interested in your previous experience but only as long as it is put in context of their needs.

Do you have a 'know-it-all' attitude? Do you talk about your previous experience and assume you will do the same thing in your new role regardless? Are you open to new ideas? Do you see another person's needs and point of view? Action: Talk in terms of the prospective employer's needs and relate your experience to these needs.

The Irrational Attitude

Irrational people give themselves away because they lack self-confidence. When asked about certain subjects, their argument falls apart and then they have an even bigger problem.

Do you have an irrational attitude? Are you under qualified for the job you are applying for? Are you perhaps setting your goals far too high from where you are at the moment? Are you reaching for standards that you couldn't possibly achieve right now and therefore you will always fail? Or are you applying for jobs for which you are overqualified and therefore, not giving yourself a chance to reach your full potential? Action: Try to sort out in your own mind, what you want from your career and be realistic in your approach.

The Sloppy Attitude

The sloppy person either can't be bothered to get it right or isn't even aware that he or she is slipping up.

Do you have a sloppy attitude? Do you have a good CV and interview manners? Do you have a conscience for good hygiene and appearance or are you inclined to be lax in these areas? Do you consider your family circumstances while taking decisions – Will this choice of career be a good move for just you or for the whole family? Have you considered how long hours and excessive time away from home or relocating will affect you all? The interviewer will ask you and you will be expected to have given it some thought. Action: Identify what the problem is, and if you don't know ask a close friend or a career advisor or ring up the interviewer and be brave enough to ask. Try to listen to what was said and reflect upon it. Is it true or false? If false, ignore it and think no more about it, but if true, be brave and sort it out.

Interview Preparation

The Non-Conformist Attitude

Employers claim that non-conformity is an automatic reason for rejection. Candidates need to demonstrate to a prospective employer that they can and will follow basic instructions and requests.

Do you have a non-conformist attitude? Are you letting yourself down because you are not submitting information that the employer is asking for, i.e., filling in the form badly, arriving late for an interview or giving your preferred answer to the question asked? Action: Whether you like it or not, remember that the only rule of job hunting is to do what the employer asks and do what you say you will do. After all, you want the job and it is not your job to criticise or change the requirements. You will have the chance to demonstrate your flair and originality at the interview and to assess whether you will fit in with the organisation. All the negative attitudes highlighted above have a higher failure rate than success rate.

Positive Attitudes

> *Take time out for yourself * Look for the good in yourself and others * Talk about positive things.*

Employers want people to have a decisive, visionary and positive attitude; an attitude that will add value to the company. Candidates need to be aware of their capabilities, strengths and weaknesses and be able to express themselves both verbally and in writing. Remember however, that you don't have to be too slick or perfect in your approach. This in itself is often viewed as a negative attribute because it looks too false as if you have rehearsed your performance so much that you reel it off pat, and it is therefore, hard to see how much of it is you or the puppet in motion.

A Visionary Attitude

A visionary approach is key to your success. It is not enough to muddle through from task-to-task and from job-to-job. Employers need conviction that you are the right person for a particular job and to convince them you need to believe in yourself first. A vision is having a clear idea of your future, your long and short-term goals; knowing what motivates and drives you; having an awareness of your current skills and capabilities and knowing what you need to develop and learn in order to propel you forward.

If you don't know where you want your career to go, look in the papers and talk to friends, colleagues and contacts. What jobs excite you and who do you aspire to be? You will learn to be imaginative and creative in planning your future. You will see the value of paying attention to your inner thoughts. To reach your full potential, you will need to take time to establish your vision for your career by networking, shadowing, training or seeking a mentor. By removing all limitations and being dedicated to your vision, you could achieve far more than you ever dreamed possible.

A Positive Attitude Helps

A positive attitude will help you to secure success. No one wants to hire a tired, negative person. So, if you show signs of being worn down by life, sort things out. A video of a practice interview will show whether your answers are defensive or whether you are promoting yourself. If you feel positive about yourself, you will influence the environment positively and employers will want to hire you. Follow the guidelines below if you wish to create a positive attitude.

- Take time out for yourself. Whether it is first thing in the morning or last thing at night, give yourself time off. Do things you enjoy and remember if you build a positive attitude in one area it will spill over into another area.

- Look for the good in yourself and others. Nobody is perfect, but everyone has good qualities. You are a unique person and you are important. Learn to appreciate what is good about yourself. Likewise, give others enthusiastic praise and appreciation. If you are jealous and bitter towards others, then be aware that this could be a sign that you wish to be like them. If you try, you can be.
- Talk about positive things. Positive thoughts create positive feelings and help you to build worthy relationships with others. People ask you every day, 'How are you?' But the key is in your answer – is it a half-hearted one or a negative one? Convey a positive message instead.

Act now on your resolution. You want action now, not in a year's time. So don't put off taking that necessary action now.

A Realistic Attitude

The following will help you develop a realistic approach to your career and this in turn will lead to greater job satisfaction. A realistic attitude is:
- Selling yourself to your highest potential
- Making all those important job and career decisions that most job hunters get concerned about

If you set your mind on it, you can secure a job that you will enjoy and that will enhance your abilities and your income. Thus, work can be transformed from a daily drudge into a fulfilling experience. The benefit for you is that you can have that special job rather than just fantasising about it. Give it a try and remember that in order to avoid disaster and disappointment in job hunting, you have just got to keep it and never put it off until tomorrow, what you can do today.

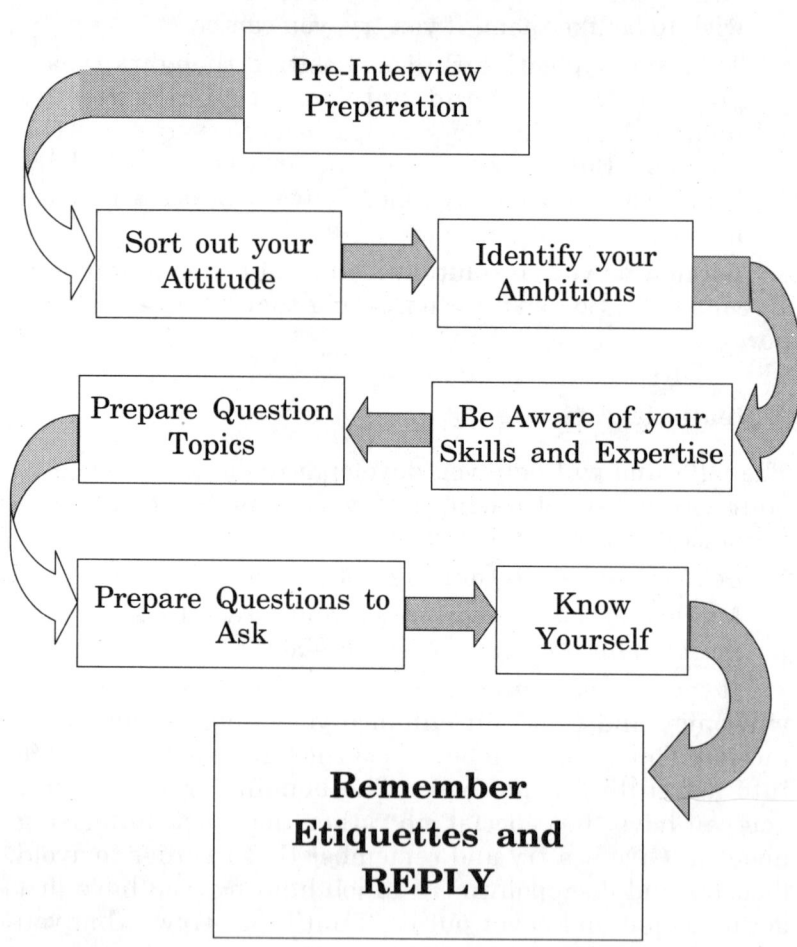

Self-Appraisal

Read the following questions and see what you have to offer an employer. Then, if appropriate, you can refer to these points in response to the interviewer's questions.

- **Are you hardworking?** Do you give your job your all or do the hours set? Do you waste time chatting or stretch your lunch hour? Do you have tangible results to show for your efforts?
- **Are you disciplined?** What do you do in terms of meeting your tasks? Get on with it and work until you have finished? Or put things off, feel guilty about it and then complete the job in an almighty rush?
- **Are you organised?** Are you tidy or messy? Do you plan things and carry it out? Would you be able to find something somebody wanted? Or is it in a cupboard or drawer somewhere, among all the mess? Do you write things down or rely upon your memory? What about missing appointments and forgetting deadlines? Do you constantly have to work extra hours in order to catch up?
- **How good a leader are you?** Are you a born leader, inspiring others to do what you ask of them? Can you judge characters? How assertive are you? Are you diplomatic and tactful or do you hurt others because you don't think before you speak? Are you greedy and take all the praise for a job well done or do you share the credit?
- **What about your energy level?** Do you suffer from tiredness and have to take time out to catch up on your sleep? Do you need to sleep late on your day offs in order to feel human again? Do you take to regular exercise and holidays? Or do you have to call the office when you are on holiday?
- **Are you competitive?** You want to be ahead of your peers and colleagues but do you work to achieve towards it? Do you constantly improve your skills? Have you got your goals, which you are working towards – perhaps, a raise in salary, a promotion or a senior management role?

Or are you a dreamer, hoping that someone somewhere will discover you and your attributes?
- **Are you a planner?** Do you take control and manage your own career or are you constantly hoping that someone will do this for you? Do you set goals for yourself and stick to them or do you resist any form of planning?

Overcome Fears

It is not only you but most people fear attending interviews. For beginners and people who have had bad experiences in the past, it can be especially nerve-racking. It then seems to get even more daunting. It is not that they don't want the job because they do; it is just that the process to achieve it is such a big hurdle. The actual thought of attending the interview creates panic. Negative thoughts take over, for example:

- Will I get the job?
- Will I be good enough?
- Will I be able to answer all the questions?

It is normal to be nervous and it often works to your advantage because you are sharper. However, it is necessary to strike a balance between being nervous and being gripped by panic. This chapter demonstrates how to calm the nerves and how to prepare, so that you can attend an interview with confidence and conviction.

Never forget that interviewers are looking for someone to fill their vacancy. Being selected for an interview means that you stand as good a chance as anyone of being chosen. In fact, interviewers want to choose someone from their shortlist, and that someone could be you. Interviewers are there to draw out the best from candidates; they are not there to trick, embarrass or ridicule them.

So, remember that interviewers want the best from candidates and you want to be the best. An interview is a performance. It is your chance to shine through and sell your special qualities and skills. So prepare beforehand and it shouldn't be such an ordeal after all; it might perhaps even turn out to be an enjoyable experience.

Interview Or Job

Before looking at how to steady interview nerves, consider first whether you are nervous about the interview or about the job itself. For example, I had a client who came to me after a particular difficult interview experience. He was at first very reticent to divulge any information about 'that awful interview'. Once I gained his trust, he told me that he had never considered himself a nervous person, but once he was in the interview room his nerves took over. The questions had been firing for about ten minutes and it was then that he noticed the interview panel looking at him very strangely. It was at this point he realised that although he thought he was talking because the words were buzzing round his head, he wasn't actually saying anything because he couldn't move his mouth. The muscles had frozen and stiffened due to extreme nerves. I have only come across this once. However, on working to resolve this situation, the person realised that the reason he got so nervous at interviews was because he was chasing the wrong kind of jobs. He didn't want the job he was being considered for, hence silence gripped him at the interview. The outcome was that he realigned his career; applied for jobs he wanted, worked upon his interview performance and no longer dreaded the interview. Thus, he landed himself in the right kind of job.

3

ASSESS YOURSELF BEFORE AN INTERVIEW

How To Assess Yourself

Remember that there is more to work than merely having a job. It must be a job that fulfils you and rewards you for your efforts. So, you need to assess whether this is a job that you would be proud to have, whether it offers you long-term potential and whether it is in line with your career aspirations.

Common Worries

Everyone has their own worries and concerns about attending interviews. Commonly, people may suffer from a fear of:
- Meeting new people
- The attention resting upon them
- Travelling to a different location
- Being asked difficult questions
- Failure – again
- Being embarrassed or intimidated
- Having to perform
- Being over or under-dressed

Knowing what gives you the jitters or wobbles means that you are halfway to resolving it; at least you know what to work on putting right. If you do not identify with any of the above points, but still get very nervous about attending interviews, work through the points on overcoming fears. It can do you no harm and may help to steady those nerves anyway.

Calm Your Nerves

> * Have Faith In Your CV * Focus On Others * Be Aware Of The Environment * Forget The Significance Of The Interview * Tell Yourself You'll Enjoy * Rehearse

Calm your nerves by following and practising the points listed below. At first it may seem unnatural, but with practice it will become easier.

Have Faith In Your CV

Since you wrote your CV, therefore it should be good! The CV or application form is the script for the interview. Everything the employer knows about you till date is written down on the paper in front of him. Before the interview, read through it several times and have faith in it. The types of questions asked will be determined by the content of the CV. Once at the interview there is *no* harm in repeating some of the information in the CV. Concentrate on the question and reply by making yourself look a winner. Focus on the positive and don't be shy. Believe in yourself and the interviewer will believe in your abilities as well. While delivering the answers, sit comfortably and try not to fiddle too much or make too many gestures. It is not necessary to go into an act but try to make an impression upon the interviewer. Present a friendly but business-like manner.

You don't want to be locked in a permanent grin, so the occasional smile is what is required.

Above all, remember that you are in the marketplace, so sell yourself.

Focus On Others

To calm the nerves, stop thinking about yourself and how you feel. This will only make matters worse, as the more nervous you feel the more nervous you will become. So, try to practice focusing on others if you feel panicky. How are the people around you behaving? While waiting for the interview, watch the people, the receptionist and the employees. They are unlikely to be nervous as they are doing a normal day's work just as you usually do. On meeting the interviewer, focus on him or her rather than yourself. Listen to what he or she is saying, how he or she is coping and reacting and remember that he or she might be as nervous as you are, especially if it is the first time in the interviewer's chair. So, never underestimate other people with possible nervousness, as it will affect their behaviour too.

Be Aware Of The Environment

Take an interest in where you are – the building you are in, the interview room, the lighting, temperature, the decor and also the noise levels. Sometimes interviewers break the ice by asking, "Are you warm enough?" or something similar and very often, the nervous reply is, "I don't know". To avoid a stupid throwaway comment that could haunt you throughout the interview, be conscious of your surroundings. Ask yourself whether you would be happy working in this environment.

Forget The Significance Of The Interview

Try to forget that this is an interview and that you are facing an interview board. Forget the fact that you need the job to pay the bills or that, this job is a one-in-a-million opportunity or the job of a lifetime or if you are being interviewed for a higher course of learning, for which this interview is your last. If you do not succeed in this one you are left no where. Thinking alone, on these lines, affects performance. It makes it difficult to concentrate and to be relaxed and above all, it increases pressure. Sportsmen often say that they try to forget that they are competing in the Olympics, the Wimbledon Final or the FA Cup Final. Instead, they think that it is just another match, another game – the game they enjoy and live for. Do the same in the job interview. Forget about how you are coming over and whether you will be offered the job. Instead, concentrate on answering the questions and think about what is happening in the present. Be yourself and let your personality shine through. Don't be tempted to think about the outcome, as it will only interfere with your performance.

Tell Yourself You'll Enjoy

A positive mental attitude creates positive thoughts, which turn into positive actions. Tell yourself you will enjoy the whole interview and it will come true. It is, after all, only another business conversation, something which you do every day of your life. Learn from your past mistakes and see the whole process as a learning process. Put into practice what you learned from the last interview and remember that 'practice makes perfect'.

Rehearse

It is crucial to practice being interviewed, as it will dramatically increase your performance. An interview is an unnatural set-up and can cause people to behave differently. A client of mine was totally unaware, until she saw herself on video, that once under pressure she would point and shake her finger at the person asking the questions – somewhat putting off for the interviewer. In such a case, the interviewer might focus totally on the quirky movements rather than on what the person is saying. Are you aware of how you come across? It is common for people to wave their arms or legs, nod their head, fiddle with coins in their pocket, close their eyes or swing on the chair. Seeing yourself in action can be quite a surprise.

Practice as though you are being interviewed. Get someone you trust, either a partner or a friend, to interview you. It is best to allocate 15-20 minutes, so that the person can ask you a continuous flow of questions. This allows you to relax once the initial feelings of self-consciousness have worn off. Try to persuade the person to prepare the questions, as this makes the situation more realistic and creates the element of surprise for you. Lastly, either borrow or hire a camcorder so that you can video the dummy interview.

Before looking at the tapes, get the person to give their honest opinion. Listen and take their advice, then take a look for yourself. Is this the real you on video? Watch the interview several times to allow the initial shock to wear off. You may need to do some work on your posture and your body movements. Above all, note your facial expressions. What do they tell you? Are you frowning or staring, and where is that smile? Listen to your voice. What is the pitch like? Is it flat and boring or raised and squeaky? Try to avoid falling into the habit of raising your voice at the end of each sentence, as this portrays a lack of confidence and makes it appear as if you are seeking the listener's approval to what is being said. Subtly lowering your voice at the end of a sentence, gives an authoritative and much more convincing touch.

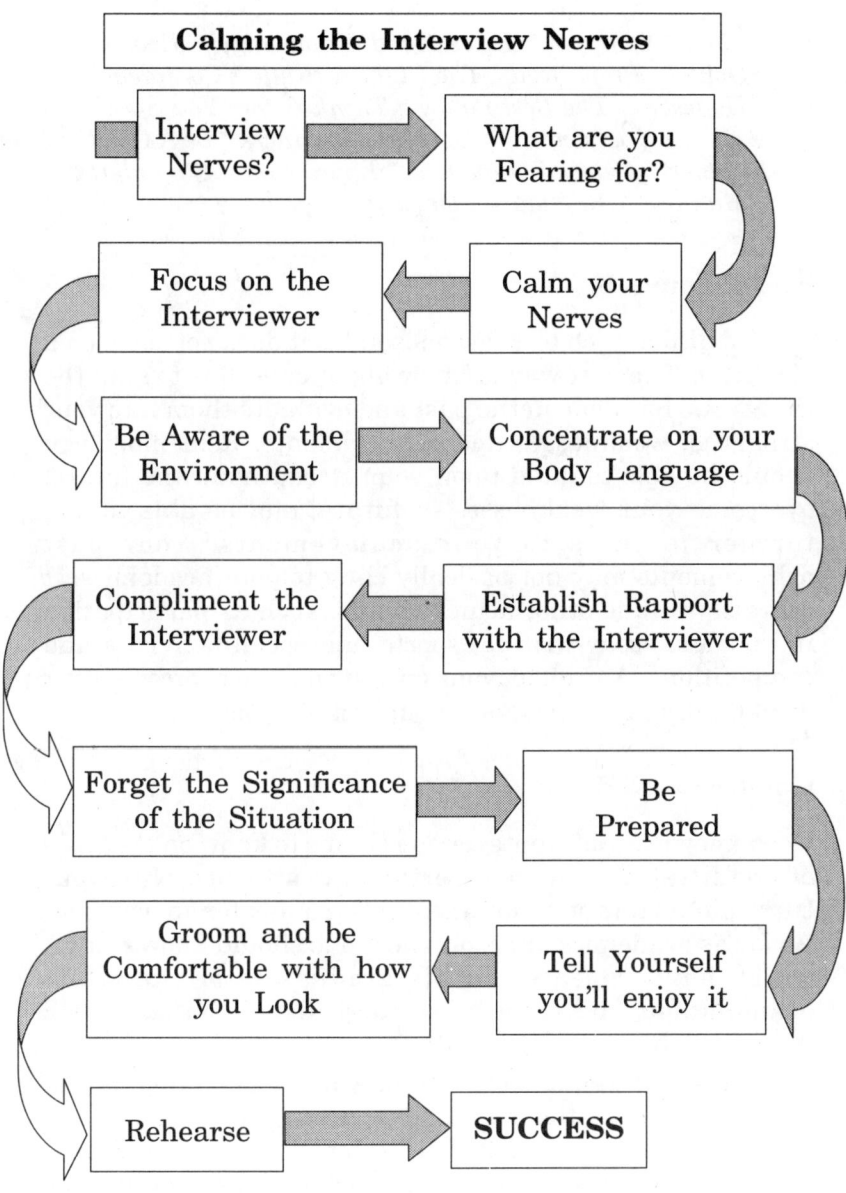

Some Guiding Factors

* Know Yourself * Have Good Knowledge * Reason
* Don't be Prejudiced * The Right Attitude * Confidence
* Honesty Is The Best Policy * Think Before You Speak
A winning personality * Speaking Manners * Be A Good
Listener * General etiquettes * Expression * Stay alert
* Manners * Be Smart * Dress appropriately

Know Yourself

It is a difficult job to know oneself, as it does not come on a platter. The best way to know about oneself is to scan the things one has done in the past and evaluate them into your strengths, weaknesses and achievements. Remember you should be able to build upon your strengths in the future, overcome your weaknesses in future; and be able to add further feathers to your achievements. Your past achievements may not basically cling to your academics; it can also include other achievements, such as participation in debates, essay-writing, sports and social activities and competitions. Any endeavour on your part to overcome your weaknesses in the past is certainly a plus point.

Good Knowledge

Good knowledge of whatever one claims to know on the basis of one's testimonials and certificates attached with your curriculum vitae or resume is a *sine qua non* for an aspirant. As far as academics are concerned, one should know things, which have appeared in his graduation or the latest examinations and other extra-curricular activities that a person might have participated in.

It may be remembered that a person's ability is not measured only by the marks he secured in his academics, it also concerns the knowledge he has of the subjects and their application to present day situations and he should be able to reason difficulties and problems with the methods of his academics. Thus, it is emphasised that the need to know the subjects of academics is to understand them in common situations and their applications and therefore, cramming in no way helps.

So, the emphasis should be to just revise the books and understand basic concepts rather than reading the complete book from cover to cover. The interviewers are not there to bully you with very difficult situations provided you don't make yourself susceptible to it.

Once you have your concepts clearly embedded in your mind, the next step demands of you to consider how these concepts can be applied in real life situations.

As we have discussed earlier, the organisation is trying to locate 'the real you', the person as a whole. It is but natural to ask questions that may not relate to your skills or specialisation. Interviewers are equally, likely, to ask questions concerning the interviewee's interests and hobbies, to gather information about one's personality. If you say that you are fond of films, you should be aware of the leading stars, the latest releases, etc. If you say that you are fond of Indi-pop, you should have substantial knowledge of various singers and albums. If you say you are interested in gardening, you must know various aspects of gardening, fruits, flowers and plants with changing seasons. If you are casually interested, just don't say so or make it explicit that you are interested in a hobby say reading, provided you get time and knowledge of the latest launches, which is limited.

Whatever the status of a person, one ought to know the general happenings in the society, country and the world. You should be quite regular in reading the newspaper, a business magazine and some leading magazines to brush up your knowledge on the latest developments in all fields.

Reasoning

Whatever your deductions of an incident or happening should be based on sound reasoning, supported by facts. Logical conclusions make you a fit person for a job. Sometimes, interviewers are likely to put up a situation asking you to analyze it. The given situation may be totally a new concept, which you may not be aware of. You should not say what would be your mode of conduct or what you would do. Reason it out and say that you would do it in a certain fashion because of certain facts.

It needs practice. Whatever situations you come across in general life or through newspapers, build upon the situation to deduce various facts, real and imaginary both, and reason out a logical conclusion flowing out from such a build-up. Suppose, you read about *Hizbul Mujahideen's* offer to cease fire in the Kashmir valley, ask yourself, if you were the Prime Minister or the minister in-charge, how you would have interacted or dealt with the situation. Note down your pros and cons points and match them with what various personalities and journalists have said and improve upon your facts. It may sound rubbish but is a truth – that one should not base one's conclusions on the views of a single politician because most of their views are in line with the benefits to their party and electoral gains; and therefore, not much of an advantage. Whatever conclusions you have reached, discuss it with friends and peers to see the logic in them.

Don't be Prejudiced

While gauging out conclusions, don't fail to see the reasons put forward or hidden, of the parties involved in the incident or ideology. Take for example, the case of a strike of police personnel in Bihar. Your reasoning should include arguments of both—the striking personnel as well as the government besides the resultant problem faced by common men on the street. It is important because in common situations, reactions generally are based upon personal interests rather than the interest of the society as a whole. I can cite an example of a person when a staunch opponent of V.P. Singh voted for him in the election. When asked, he coolly said that he was still against all the politics of V.P. Singh except one,

Assess Yourself Before an Interview

that of one's rank—one pension for retired defence personnel and he was an affected party. You should try to know the truth behind the facts or statements and should not conclude on the basis of facts, which are superficial in essence.

The Right Attitude

The above discussion follows that the attitude of a person vis-à-vis various situations should be based on sound judgments. It is not that the interviewer is trying to know your conclusions; what he is trying to know is the process by which you reached a certain conclusion on the basis of the facts. An interviewee should not be a staunch supporter of an ideology. His approach should be flexible. Suppose, after you have come to a deduction, and the interviewer brings out a new situation, don't hesitate to change your conclusions based on that fact. It would show your flexibility in changing situations.

Confidence

No candidate can face an interview successfully if he is nervous and shaky. It is not easy for a boy who is shy and timid to appear calm and confident at the interview. No profitable habit is easily established. It may take some blasting to get rid of the old one that is holding you back. The secret of getting rid of a habit is to establish a new one in its place and continue to use the new habit until it has displaced the old one. If you are shy or timid, it devolves upon you to set yourself free. This can be done by practising the very opposite of being shy, i.e., habits of courage and confidence. If you have a strong will to win you will get the way. Lack of confidence arises out of your shortcomings. Try to know them and get rid of them. Try to be sociable and get opportunities to mix with different types of people with different habits. Do visit different places in order to get in touch with different types of people. This will go a long way in getting rid of your shyness and nervousness The more experience you gather, the more confidence you will develop. You should not be a mere bookworm. In your free time you should participate in different types of activities, physical as well as mental. Taking part in games and sports will give you a lot of courage and confidence. Nature has blessed every individual with certain positive traits, which every individual has to discover for himself or herself, and must chart out his or her course with strong confidence.

An employer is interested in a candidate who is keen to learn and improve upon himself. Successes and failures are a part of life. Confidence comes in many ways, through clear thoughts, self-confidence; experience to have dealt with similar situations before, etc. You should be confident to say something that you think is right. Hesitating to say exudes that you are not confident enough in what you say. So be careful. This confidence can be acquired through practice. Start from trivial things in life like domestic situations, meeting strangers, etc.

Honesty Is The Best Policy

The old adage 'honesty is the best policy' holds true in this case. The interviewee should be faithful and truthful. Generally, opportunity is provided by interviewers to ask any question that may be lingering in an interviewee's mind. Be frank to discuss your hopes and desires, ambitions and aspirations. You have to show that you are the right person to fit the post. Giving a false and strained impression is going to have adverse impact upon your performance, and most of the times your false impression can also be identified by the interviewer.

While speaking about your goals, don't say intangible things, but define your ambitions in terms of goals, which are tangible and can be achieved. One needs to think over these goals himself in his mind before speaking about them so that the concept can be clear and expressed in unambiguous words. The employer wants 'the real you', and we are emphasising this again and again only to tell you that an employer wants more than a worker. He is also looking for a person with some extra qualities such as creativity, analytical skills, imagination, leadership qualities and the capability to solve and face unseen situations, instead of a mechanical worker.

Think Before You Speak

The adage 'think thrice before you speak' fits best the occasion of an interview, for a wrong or misconceived answer can spoil the whole show and give a misplaced impression having bearing on the final outcome. It is not only desirable to develop the habit of expressing one's ideas correctly and explicitly; it should be relevant to the question or discussion posed.

Personality

A winning personality is the keystone in the arch of success. Your personality is the greatest asset you will ever have. More than anything else it is your personality that will tilt the favour of the interviewers to your side. Your personality is the sum total of your qualities physical, mental and spiritual. Personality does not consist only of handsome features or a well-built body. Popularly we use the term personality to describe those traits, which make people attractive or unattractive to other people. Psychologists have used the term personality to denote considerably more than physical attractiveness. Their definition of personality includes physique, appearance, intelligence, aptitudes and an individual's characteristic ways of conducting himself in everyday situations. It also includes the individual's spiritual make-up, his outlook towards life and his approach to the problems of life. All these contribute to the impression, which the candidate makes on the interviewers.

Generally, the interviewer engages the examinee in conversation, permitting him to do most of the talking. An experienced interviewer will gain many valuable insights into the individual's personality traits from his expressed interests and ambitions, his dress code, his manner of expression, hesitations, emotions, blockings and conclusions. The way a candidate opens the door, enters the room, wishes the interviewers, the way he draws the chair and sits down, his facial expressions, all these are embodied in the candidate's personality. Not all the traits of our character are inborn or God-gifted. It is up to the candidate to develop in himself such traits, which are pleasing, forceful and dynamic, and then alone he can impress people favourably.

Truly winning personalities can be built only by putting in hard labour and paying the required price. They cannot just get it. Suppose you want to become a police officer, then ask yourself this question: "What can I add to my personality to become a successful police officer? What are the characteristic qualities that are required in that department?" You can list the requirements and get a clear picture of what is expected of you. Find out what is lacking there and what you must put in. The nearer you can bring your personality up to the requirements that will meet these wants, the bigger gainer you are.

Those who possess a positive outlook towards life – hold balanced views about things controversial, explore the good in the jungle of evil are large-hearted and generous, behave with courtesy and decorum, shun mannerisms and are straight-forward in self-presentation, do not allow themselves to be unsettled by adverse criticism by others can certainly make a mark on those who are deficient in these traits. A positive personality is an asset which one must develop in order to be successful not only at the battle of an interview but also in the complex struggle of life.

Speaking Manners

While it is of utmost importance to observe speaking manners, it is absolutely necessary to avoid any such mannerisms that may look uncivilised. One should be polite but firm and should use standard language to answer the questions. Waving hands here and there, using slang's, passing personal comments, using inconsiderate, sharp and uncharitable remarks about others are entirely shunned. One should be particularly cautious about comments on present or former employer, colleagues, or business associates, especially the personal ones.

While it is prudent not to talk too much, it is also advisable not to answer the questions in simple 'yes' or 'no'.

Be A Good Listener

A person, who listens to others properly, can answer prudently. So, always allow the interviewer to finish speaking before answering. It is bad manners to interrupt. While listening, one's gestures should be such to convey his interest in the talk. Be attentive.

Etiquettes

General etiquettes must be observed that best suit the occasion. Walk and sit properly. Do not place your hands on the table or chair arms. Avoid flushing out your cigarette pack or tobacco and light. The worst situation would be to throw out match sticks and ash on the floor on not finding an ashtray. Say simply, "No, thanks" if offered tea or eatables provided it is stated categorically, "Have a cup of coffee, Mr … ." Speak softly during the course of the interview. Don't laugh loudly. Do not move your limbs to create unnecessary sounds. Do not change your stance too often, especially during interviews that are short.

Expression

The way a candidate expresses his thoughts and ideas is very much responsible in deciding his fate at the interview. It is by your expression that you reveal your thinking power. If your thoughts and ideas are clear you will be able to express them clearly in an impressive language otherwise not. If your thoughts are confused or ambiguous you cannot express them in a clear and convincing way. You cannot impress the interviewer by your expression if you speak in an affected style or talk in a pedantic way. Your answers should be short, precise, well-worded and spoken in a clear and pleasing tone. Do not try to elaborate your answers unnecessarily. Give only what is wanted. In every case, every word should be clear; your voice should be neither too loud nor too mild. Your face should wear a natural and cheerful smile and your tone should be very pleasing. Even correct answers given in a harsh and irritating tone is apt to produce an unfavourable impression on the interviewer or interviewers. Never try to enter into an argument with the interviewer even when you find that he is in the wrong. If you are wrong admit it quickly and without any hesitation. Never interrupt the interviewer even if you are tempted to do so. Speak up only when he finishes. Exclusive attention paid to the interviewer is very important.

Alertness

The candidate should be very alert at the time of the interview. He should take minimum time in understanding the question of the interviewer. Sometimes the interviewer interrupts the candidate while he is answering a question and puts entirely a different type of question. In such a case, the candidate should forget the previous question completely and give all his attention to the new question in order to grasp it and answer it successfully and that too, without showing any signs of irritation for not being allowed to express your full view regarding the previous question. Thus the candidate should show his preparedness to accept new challenges. You will not impress the interviewer favourably if to every new question put to you, you say "I beg your pardon, Sir," that shows your lack of attention and alertness and this irritates the interviewer.

If you do not know the answer of the question admit your ignorance promptly and politely and that will do. Surely,

Assess Yourself Before an Interview 51

you are not going to lose on account of this. Nobody is expected to know each and everything in the world. You must show to the interviewer that you are paying attention to him and you are taking full interest in his questions. You must not give the impression that you are taking it lightly. Your alertness in responding to his questions will show that you are quite serious about the interview and you have a real liking for the job.

Manners

A person is generally judged by his manners. Your manners show your status, breeding and background. If you are asking for a good job or a status in life you should cultivate good and pleasing manners from a very early stage. You cannot adopt the best manners before the interviewers unless you have acquired them after a long practice. When you go for an interview your manners are revealed in your posture, walk, the way you enter the room, how you wish the interviewers, face them, and speak to them and so on. When you appear before the interviewer or a board of interviewers, you have to prove that you are a well-mannered person.

When you enter the interview room you have to stand properly before the interviewers, your hands and head in the proper position. There should be nothing abnormal in your way of standing but the impression should be that of a genuine interest and attention required for the interview. You should appear neither too bold nor too cowering. You should be cautious about your standing position at the end of the interview and you should be prepared for the handshake, if there is going to be any but on no account should you take the initiative to shake hands yourself. You have not to keep standing even for a moment when the interview is over and should walk gently out of the room.

Your manners are also revealed in your sitting position before the interviewers. Do not show your nervousness by moving your hands unnecessarily or touching the things kept on the table. Your hands should lie on the table in a relaxed position. You should not appear staring at the interviewers or move your head this way and that way looking at things placed in the room. You should be perfectly composed and normal without showing any sign of shakiness or nervousness.

Your manner of speaking should be pleasing and impressive. Every word should be clear and distinct. Do not speak hurriedly and loudly. Words should be properly pronounced and stressed when needed and there should be a proper rhythm in your speech. Your answers should be precise, relevant and to the point, neither too short nor too long. You should not move your body unnecessarily while speaking. While giving an answer you should face the interviewer who is putting the question to you and do not turn your eyes to the other interviewers unnecessarily. If you are unable to answer a question, do not feel embarrassed or nervous. Just accept your ignorance very politely and wait for the next question.

There is a term body language, which speaks louder than the words you speak. Unnecessary movement of hands, head, shaking the legs while sitting, smattering beyond intelligibility, smiling or laughing without any valid reason, thumping the table to emphasise a point, sitting or standing in an abnormal way, all these things must be avoided. Constant practice can enable you to shake off these characteristics, if unfortunately; they have become a part of your personality.

Smartness

To catch the attention of the interviewers, the candidate should be smartly dressed. The first impression created by the candidate on the interviewers will be by the dress. In this case, you should remember the universal advice given by Polonius to Lacerates in Shakespeare's play *'Hamlet'*:

Be not expressed in fancy, rich not gaudy; for the apparel often proclaimed the man. A smart dress does not necessarily mean a costly dress. First of all, your clothes should be properly tailored and should fit you well. The shade of the cloth of your suit counts a lot. You must make a difference between a suit for a marriage or a party and a suit for the interview.

The interview is a serious and solemn affair. Your dress, therefore, must be sober, simple and pleasing. There should be nothing showy about it and you should not be conscious of it at the time of the interview. You should also take into account the weather and season at the time of the interview while choosing your dress. While a woolen suit may be worn if it is winter, a blue shirt and pant may do in summer. You should feel quite at ease in your clothes. Your shoes should be polished well. You should be well shaved and your hair should be well combed without looking too oily. You should look natural and poised without looking bold or shaky. The only aim is to show yourself at your best and that too without much a do at the time of interview. The effort should be towards showing that it is your natural way of doing or saying things.

Dress

Image and appearance matter! Being well-groomed shows self-respect and value for the people you meet and work with. It is not necessary to spend obscene amounts of money on the best clothes, but to buy what you can afford, to dress in accordance with the company style and to pay attention to grooming.

First impression is the last impression, and in case of an interview, it is the dress that plays a vital role in forming an initial impression by the interviewer. Dressing up for interviews is rather tricky; there can be no hard and fast rules here. Some suggestions: Think of the usual dress of a person who is doing the same work for which you are being interviewed. Barring professions where the employee (for example nurses or hotel staff, etc.) wears a uniform you would do well to wear a dress that is normally worn by the person while on job, only a little more formal because if you are seen to be comfortable in those clothes it is a positive point and in your favour. For example, if you were going for the job of a sales representative it would be better to wear a tie and light-coloured sober clothes. This is the dress that sales persons generally wear. Similarly, if you are a lady and the job for which you have applied demands that you wear trousers it would be good that you wore trousers for the interview. This will demonstrate that you are comfortable in trousers. If you are going for back-office jobs like accounting, call centre, etc., you would do well to wear casual, loose-fitting comfortable clothes in which you can stay on work for long hours.

Always keep in mind that the interview does not start after you have occupied the chair. Your assessment starts the moment you make an entry into the premises of the organisation. Though not always, but many times your conduct while you approach the reception may also be observed. This is especially true in smaller organisations where the receptionist may also be part of the administrative set up. The moment you enter the interview room, your body language, your attire, the way you walk towards the waiting chair and the way you occupy it, will leave an impact on the interviewer. It is unfortunate but true that most of us have preconceived notions about people. Most interviewers will decide in that first minute whether the candidate fits into the post or not. He may change his mind depending on how your interview goes subsequently, but a considerable number of rejections are made during those first few minutes.

There exists some difference of opinion regarding dress, but most agree that the best dress for a formal occasion like an interview should be formal. What is a formal or informal dress is again a point of debate. Different posts may demand different dress codes. For example, an interview for the post of a *jyotish* translator or an astrologer or a priest may call for a different dress than what we may call formal.

An informal dress may be a traditional or conventional or religious dress, but in case one wears one such informal dress, one should be ready to bear the brunt of questions on the dress itself, and prove beyond doubt the reasons of adoring such a dress. Inability to make the interviewer agree in favour of such a dress is certainly going against the candidate, resulting in loss of some vital marks that may make all the difference between a successful and an unsuccessful candidate.

The woman candidates have varied choices to make as far as dress is concerned; from *sari* to *salwar kameez* to skirts to jeans. But choice for male candidates for a formal occasion is quite limited. A trouser with shirt and tie or a suit with a tie is the preferable choices depending upon the time of season and time and place of the interview.

In India however, the safest thing for men is a shirt-trousers-tie combination in summer and tie with jacket in winters. For women, except in customer service jobs, it is safest to wear a decent *sari* or *salwar suit*. For ladies in customer service jobs, it is better to wear loose-fitting trousers.

The basic thing to remember is that you should not be too unconventional or shocking. It is better to go along with the local norms of decent behaviour. No employer would be keen to take an employee who is dramatically different from the routine. For example, in traditional industries in Mumbai or Bangalore, trousers may be much more acceptable for ladies than in Delhi, Chennai or Lucknow.

However, no one can prescribe a strict dress code for an interview. You have to take into account local cultural issues and the type of job applied for. Your own comfort level with the dress is also very important. If you are the conservative types, and have never worn jeans or trousers; it would be better to wear the type of dress you are more comfortable with, unless a specific desired dress code is associated with the industry.

Light colour shirts with somewhat darker contrasting trousers make you look more decent than bright dark colour shirts.

In any case, one should avoid wearing hanky-panky clothes like jeans and t-shirts. The knot of neck-tie should be in fashion. Clothes should be clean and well-ironed. Shoes should be shining. Hair should be well-groomed.

While giving the interview, a person should look attractive and impressive in the dress. The dress should fit the person well. Also, a natural smile should play on the lips. Cosmetics can be used but strong fragrances should better be avoided. Make-up in the case of women should not be heavy and dark. It should be light and should not give an extravagant look.

Most important of all, a person should be comfortable in his or her dress. Choose your dress according to your stature, complexion, and weather. Whenever in doubt as regards dress, stick to the conventional formal dress code, which should appeal to the interviewer.

Having dressed for the occasion, stand in front of a full-length mirror and view yourself critically. If the mirror compliments you on your dress, the smart and confident 'you' is ready to face the interview board.

Dress for your interview in line with the company's image. To get it right, start by looking at the advertisement, application packs and company brochure. What image does the company portray? A glossy image might mean they want a classy, formal style and a badly photo-copied pamphlet might mean that they don't pay attention to their image and presentation at all. However, before forming your opinion, it is advisable to check out the company further. Before the interview, visit the building from the outside and watch the staff as they leave for lunch. If you can, go inside the building in order to get a better look. Try to pick a day in the middle of the week as some companies have a casual friday policy.

So, research will show you whether a suit, a creative outfit or a casual approach is required. Then customise your clothes specifically to the particular company.

A client of mine underestimated the value of a visit and as a result she missed out on the job. She modified her usual 'stand upright' hairstyle for the interview and wore more formal clothes than usual. "It worked against me," she told

Assess Yourself Before an Interview

me, "because when I arrived I realised to my disappointment that my usual hairstyle and clothing was far more in keeping with the company image."

However, experiences suggest that while attending an interview, always dress formally. This would mean a lounge suit and tie for men and dresses and *saris* for women. The type of dress reflects your personality, values and character. You must realise that the interviewers' eyes are very critical. They are required to summarise, in the short period of the interview, your character and values through the visual and oral data you provide. One of the vital sources of information towards this summary is your grooming. Let me take you on a head to foot checklist of what I mean by proper grooming.

MAN	WOMAN
BODY: Ensure that you are clean and smell fresh. Before attending interview take a bath. If in doubt, do the sniff test under your arm pits?	**BODY:** Ensure that you are clean and smell fresh. Before attending interview take a shower. If in doubt, do the sniff test under your arm pits?
ODOUR: Go easy on perfume and use mild fragrances. Use good aftershave. For winters, Musk fragrance is advisable.	**ODOUR:** Go easy on perfume and use mild fragrances.
JEWELLERY: One or two rings. No bracelets or other hand gears.	**JEWELLERY:** Go easy on jewellery. Avoid bold colours and select items that enhance your outfit.
HAIR: Well cut and combed. Less oily. If a Sikh, turban should be clean and starched and tied neatly.	**HAIR:** Worn in a bun. If comfortable, hair should be left open but washed, combed and preferably styled.
FACE: Close shaven. If bearded, it should be well trimmed. Eyes, nose and ears must be clean.	**FACE:** Light make-up. No facial hair. Conservative ear rings, nose rings, if any.

MAN	WOMAN
SHIRT: Clean and well-ironed shirt. Collar must be clean especially on neck rim. Tips of collar must not be dog eared. Cuffs must be clean and well-buttoned.	**SHIRT:** Blouses to be conservative.
HANDS: Hands clean, nails well cut and clean.	**HANDS:** Hands clean. Nails well manicured. If using nail polish see that the nails are well painted. Nothing is more disagreeable than stained/chipped mismatched nail polish.
SUIT OR DRESS: Light coloured suit. Blazer combination is permissible. Should be clean and well pressed, ties must be well pressed. In hot climate, it will be in line to wear a clean, well pressed shirt, trouser and tie.	**SUIT/SARI OR DRESS:** Conservative colours. Printed saris but must be simple. Well pressed and draped. If not comfortable in a sari, wear English or Indian formal dress like Salwar Suit.
SOCKS: Preferably black or navy blue socks. White socks if spotless can also be worn.	**SOCKS:** Preferably skin coloured long socks.
SHOES: Conservative shoes preferably black to match the suit. Avoid sports or casual shoes. Avoid sports and casual shoes. Avoid wearing new shoes just purchased for the interview. You might find yourself leaving the room with a funny walk.	**SHOES:** Conservative sandals or shoes. Feet should be well manicured and clean. Can apply nail polish that matches the finger nails. Ensure that the heels are not too high. Avoid wearing new shoes just purchased for the interview. You might find yourself leaving the room with a funny walk.

Assess Yourself Before an Interview 59

In my vast experience at interviews, some of the typical grooming faults that candidates come up with in the hope of not being detected by interviewers are:
- Tie being worn with the collar button missing
- Undressed clothes
- Shirt cuffs without buttons
- Dirty nails, chipped nail polish among women
- Casual shoes or unpolished shoes

These flaws certainly distract the interviewers. It conjures up a personality that is imperfect, low in personal standards and casual.

The tips given above would certainly enhance the personality projection. A well-groomed person will exude an image of thoroughness, efficiency besides high personal standards and many other admirable qualities.

Preparation Stage

Practice Makes A Man Perfect

Interviews are not predictable. They are a spontaneous process in which the proclivities of the interviewers to a large extent, and that of the interviewee's up to a limited degree decide the course of an interview. Man is to err, so are the interviewers, but it is the interviewee who has to make an all out effort to alleviate any such possibility of committing an error.

Interviews are not difficult or a daunting phenomena, which should confuse the candidate, provided he is well prepared for the occasion. An interview is a face-to-face situation where most answers are to be delivered by the candidate, and understanding this is the important aspect. It is therefore, that stress is laid upon anticipating questions or the kind of questions and situations that may be put forward to be answered. Once anticipated questions have been listed, their probable answers can also be noted down and upgraded from time-to-time depending from organisation to organisation. This should be followed by discussing the answers with friends and peers who can help in upgrading answers, till a final answer has been reached.

These final answers are not meant to be crammed but are to be understood in their right perspective, so that suitable modifications in answers can be made in accordance with the questions finally asked in the interview. Even if an answer is known to the candidate, he should not deliver it like a parrot without blinking an eyelid, but should be spoken with proper eye contact and in a way, as if, one is formally but intimately talking.

Broadly, the questions asked in an interview can be classified into the following categories:
1. Personal questions
2. Questions pertaining to the organisation
3. Questions pertaining to academics, skills, and specialisation
4. Questions pertaining to current affairs or general knowledge, and
5. Goal-oriented questions

An interviewee should have personal knowledge. The personal knowledge entails many factors such as the personal self; academic and other qualifications; the reasons to acquire those qualifications, skills and specialisation; family and its background; the town—questions, problems, and likely solutions for the town and places where the candidate has ever lived; the organisation where the candidate has worked, its structure, purpose, achievement, and their reasons, failures and their reasons, etc. The list is long and differs from person to person. What has been mentioned in one's Curriculum Vitae (CV) should be on one's finger tips and there should appear no dichotomy in the details at the time of the interview. The candidate should be clear in his mind as to his desires, ambitions and aspirations.

The approach to be adopted in formulating one's CV should vary for different organisations.

One can brag in interviews but he should also be able to substantiate the bragging. It is basically a stage, which revolves around locating all the plus points and practising to speak about them confidently. This aspect basically includes one's achievements in various fields like sports, academics, interests, strengths, aptitude, passion, etc. It should also include one's negative attributes or weaknesses. Keep in mind to list such weaknesses in those areas where the candidate has shown some or marked improvement. The presentation of strengths and weaknesses disproportionately is going to render the CV meaningless. Where a candidate gives a long list of strengths but only one weakness showing improvement is more often than not an untruthful candidate.

The strengths and weaknesses mentioned in the CV should be on the finger tips of the candidate. While in the interview, one should speak about the facts, which he has mentioned in his CV. One should avoid giving radically different answers than those mentioned in the CV. Thus, a consistency of approach is an important aspect.

It is necessary to know the organisation one is applying for. As a pre-requisite, one should understand the advertisement in a proper way. What has been given in the interview (and what has not been) should be understood. What does the job demand, what is the salary and other fringe benefits, does the job entail travelling, are many questions that can be answered after a proper look at the advertisement. Also, take pains to see how desperately the organisation needs you or doesn't need you. What is the method of advertisement? Is it a cheap advertisement like a classified or classified display advertisement or a costly advertisement like its display on television as advertisement? Can the company afford to interview a large number of candidates or has it entrusted the job to a mediator to screen and shortlist applicants? All these factors show the importance the company attaches with the post. Also, the manner of advertisement is an important sign. If an organisation has spent considerable amount in advertising, it means that the company attaches importance to the post.

A candidate should learn to read between the lines of an advertisement. Organisations spend a lot of money on projecting their image and a candidate should try to understand the image of the company that it is trying to be projected through the advertisement, and its other advertisements in newspapers, magazines, television and other means. Is the image projected by them that of a large and smooth organisation or a smooth or professional or a rapidly expanding and changing organisation or a small or entrepreneurial organisation? If the applications have been called indirectly though an agency or a box number, one should take pains to consider why the company does not want to give its name. Also, read between the lines that introduce the company in a way to reflect the company's philosophy. Consider the size and reach of the organisation and its field of interest in products and services. These are the main factors before a person decides as to what kind of organisation he would like to work for and feel satisfied with. It sometimes happens that a person wants to work in a specific organisation, but has to work at some other place to gain experience, etc., to find himself finally, suitable for the job because lack of such experiences will be counted as a major drawback on one's part.

Once a candidate is sure of himself about the kind of organisation he would like to work for, and other benefits that come with the desired post, he needs to read the advertisement critically to see if it matches his desires and ambitions. Also, give a thought to the demands of the job that the post may entail and may or may not have stated explicitly in the advertisement. In the latter case, one would have to read between the lines. Would you be able to fulfil the criterion given in the advertisement or are your ambitions different than what the job demands? Do you have suitable qualifications and experience for the job?

Is the organisation likely to train you while on the job or in a specified institution? Does there exist a case when you may not be properly qualified for the job but have sufficient work experience or is that you are overqualified but lack experience which is desired by the company? Are you in the position to make the interview board understand that your lack of experience or qualification is not going to make any difference at all?

Generally, an advertisement lists all the qualifications that an organisation may be looking for in suitable candidates. There are no reasons to believe that the qualification possessed by you is more relevant to the job. Give it a thought, from employer's point of view whether you have any chances to be called for an interview or whether applying for the post is going to be a futile exercise, which is going to waste your time as well as that of the organisation. If you apply, you must be sure that you are in a position to convince your would-be employer about your suitability to the job.

Look for the job qualifications and classify them into essential and desirable qualifications. Generally, organisations do not allow any room in essential qualifications but can consider a wide variety of choices as far as desirable qualifications are concerned. Desirable qualifications can be dispensed with by an organisation fully or partly. Suppose the advertisement states a language qualification, which can be identified by the candidate as not directly going with the post, it would be a desirable qualification. Perhaps the candidate would have to work in such an environment where the knowledge of such a language would be required. If the candidate doesn't have a formal qualification in the language asked for, but is otherwise able to fluently interact in the language, his chances of being selected are bright, but if the job entails working in the language itself, it would be an essential qualification, and formal qualification in that field would be required. But in case of desirable qualifications, candidates do not bluff because this claim cannot be substantiated through documents and you may have to go through a test for it.

Sometimes, possession of an alternative qualification can do the job as well, but again it would depend on the necessity of the organisation and the jobs entailed by the post.

There are some cases where essential qualifications were relaxed. I remember a good case of an organisation, which relaxed essential qualification of the masters' degree in either Hindi or English with English or Hindi medium. The applicant had a third class master's degree in English and didn't have the Hindi medium. But he was selected because he had adequate work experience including translation of a number of books, which had been published.

It is possible that all organisations will not be so considerate, because in large organisations the individuals entrusted with the job of selecting applications may be in lower rung of the hierarchy and are likely to reject the application summarily.

Giving a thought to the job in advance can save you a lot of trouble. Now, think in terms of whether you would be required to work in a team or alone. Human proclivity varies from person to person. Some people like to work in a team, while some desire to tread their own way individually. Some people like to lead while others are comfortable when led. One should always give a thought to the situation one would be made to face in the new job. If the conditions are compatible in keeping with the frame of mind of the aspirant, he should go for it; else he should retreat from applying.

Salary is the main consideration coupled with job satisfaction because there are some cases where certain individuals have opted for lower salary jobs after having relinquished high salary jobs for the sake of job satisfaction. However still, salary remains the main consideration for most people. Some organisations explicitly state the salary and other fringe benefits, but other organisations simply give 'salary commensurate with age and experience', 'salary negotiable', etc., or there may not be anything mentioned.

Where these indefinite measures have been mentioned, it is to give the organisation a beneficial position and the organisation can be flexible in its approach in keeping with the age, qualification or experience of the candidate. It may also mean that they will try to settle for as little as possible or the candidate may be in a position to ask for more. There is a word of caution for an advertisement, which reads salary as 'up to' or 'the top person earned ...'. It is the attempt of the organisation to lure people to very less salary and other benefits while making them work like horses. 'A good remuneration package' has a varied meaning depending upon the organisation, and generally includes salary and other fringe benefits that normally go with the post.

It is absolutely necessary to know about the organisation and its standing before one applies for the job, provided one is not desperate for the job. Even then, a good knowledge of the organisation helps the candidate improve his chances of selection. It is also advisable to retain a copy of the application so that it can be read through before the interview.

Applying for a right job requires a person to work out his strengths, weaknesses and other requirements, in keeping with the job applied for by a person who is not suitably qualified for a post but keeps applying for a job, resulting in 'no replies' or rejection letters that is sure to break his morale. In case one is not sure of the job, one can apply in accordance with one's qualifications and experience or one should approach a consultancy. There are a lot of such consultants. One can also consult some good book on careers to know the posts one can apply for.

One should be quite sure about the subject one has studied at the graduation level. It is desirable to read through concerned books and literature and their application in real life problems, especially those that concern the job.

A person is expected to be aware of the happenings around him. Therefore, knowledge of current affairs and general knowledge is a must because there is every possibility of a candidate being asked a few questions from this field.

Current affairs and general knowledge is a vast field and no one is expected to know every thing, but a person should know the burning issues of the present and past times with analytical capacity. A person well-qualified for the job but ignorant of events around him is likely to be summarily rejected. An aptitude for general awareness also shows that the person is interested in keeping himself well-informed of what happens around him and is not likely to be caught unawares.

A person should also be aware of his future desires and ambitions, but such desires should be in keeping with the reality, and should not sound like 'castles in the air'. A realistic goal, which is achievable, is the target. A very high-flying goal can be mentioned, provided the candidate is ready to substantiate his claim to his ability to achieve such goals and make a stand for it; otherwise it may be regarded as a hallucination and can make an adverse impact upon the interviewer.

4

PROBABLE QUESTIONS

Anticipating Questions

* Describe Yourself * What Your Last Boss Was Like? * How You Fit The Job? * Where You Want To Be 10 Years From Now? * What Your Ideal Boss Would Be Like? * Questions On Inconsistencies

It may be borne in mind that the interviewer is interested in the positive 'you' who would be able to contribute to the organisation fruitfully and not prove to be a liability to the organisation, which is sure to 'fire' the candidate.

From a research of a wide variety of interviews carried out for various posts in the past, we can list some general questions that are tricky but important from the point of view of securing a job. Utmost care should be adhered to while answering such questions. A knowledge coupled with practice can bring success.

Describe Yourself

This is a tricky question. Sometimes, this question is asked in the beginning of an interview to put the candidate at ease. While answering this, keep in mind the facts already mentioned in your CV or application, and a verbose description of oneself is bound to dose the interviewer, and there is no sound reason to repeat the feats. Rather, the approach of the interviewee should be directed towards bringing out some positive traits and attributes, which has paved the way for improvement in your personal capacity or for your previous employer. It would make interviewers take active interest in you. As it is, repeating the facts already mentioned in the application is sheer folly giving an impression that you have nothing substantial to put forward.

It may be remembered that there is no absolutely perfect person in the world, and every one possesses one or the other shortcomings and you are one of them. It is good to put yourself in good light, but every time trying to give a voluminous account for a thing is a bad idea. What interviewers are looking for is a person who fits the job well, is pleasant and adaptable, is an assertive and confident person and above all, is passionate and able to interact with other employees and persons concerned with the organisation.

There is another way of probing that is, to put a question like "Tell us a story." Mind it, the interviewers are not interested in listening to a story of 'Romeo-Juliet' or how 'Khushwant Singh' became 'the honest man of the year'. They are in fact asking you to specifically tell them about your interests or hobbies which you may or may not have mentioned in your CV. Though it is true that while answering such a question, you would also need to keep with the momentum of the interview and the atmosphere prevailing in the room; the question if asked at the beginning of the interview is supposed to be taken seriously. The answer should fit the occasion well, revealing one's nature, personality and composure in a compact form.

Interviewers are generally successful persons in their own field of activities and at times develop their own specific kind of personality with firm reasoning in their behaviour and interaction. So, till an interviewee has understood or begins to understand the hidden meanings, it would be advisable to follow their words as true, and as words you can find in dictionaries without fancying otherwise.

For some interviewers, it may be just a break from their routine work and hence they prove to be talkative, while for others it may be a routine job, and most of such fellows open up for discussion depending upon the kind of the post they are interviewing. Or they may be quiet reserved and like to listen to answers in as brief a language as may be possible. When an interviewer asks the candidate to describe himself in just three words, he means it to be precisely in three words. Beginning with a voluminous account of oneself "I am a..." has already exhausted his limit. What the interviewer would like to listen is "honest, prudent, hard worker," but only in three words. But watch out, whatever traits you attribute to yourself, do not contradict it in later stages. If one of the words you have stated is 'sociability', do not give an answer at a later stage of the interview that you like to see pictures or go to excursions all by yourself. In such a case, you would have contradicted your earlier description.

An area, one needs to be careful about is "what are your strengths" and "what are your weaknesses". Don't be too hard or too soft on yourself. Weigh your strengths and weaknesses in the light of the post you have applied for. It is always easy to elaborate upon one's strengths, acting like a *'Sheikh Chilli'*; it is always tricky to answer the question on weaknesses. It would be advisable to be pragmatic than to fancy things. Search a weakness that was a major drawback in the past and discuss to show that you have mastered to overcome such negativity partially or fully. Avoid camouflaging in words and being too verbose. Also say what you did to overcome the shortcoming, and if you state that you have overcome it partially, say categorically how long it would take and how it is to be tackled in the future.

There is another way of asking this question "What do people often criticise you for?" The interviewer wants to know your weakness besides your keenness and judicious approach in pointing out your weak points. But people may not always be right. So, if you choose to put it as your strength, you need to reason it out why people are wrong and what you intend to do to alleviate such criticism. You can also quote instances when you corrected yourself depending upon the feedback you got, and also mention where you made people understand that your opinion was correct and they altered their opinion and perception. Portray yourself as a person who can change himself if a shortcoming is found or if situations so demand, and have the capacity to make people amend their views if you are correct. But this should be conveyed without any false airs about yourself.

"What would you do if you were in the post you dream of?"

Here again, the interviewer is trying to find the 'real you'. Don't brag. Don't boast. Don't fly high. Don't fancy. Be pragmatic. Be realistic. There is always a long gap between reality and dreams, and this gap can be bridged with perseverance. Dreams without due preparations is liable to prove artificial. Whatever you say, you should have facts to substantiate what you have done to achieve your dreams. And if the applied post is just a means to achieve that dream, prove it. Once a candidate who applied for the post of a territory sales manager said that he would like to be a top author and the query was, "How is this job going to help you realise that goal?" He could not answer the question. So, the advice is simple—be realistic and in consonance with the post you are applying for.

What Your Last Boss Was Like?

It is one of the trickiest questions one is likely to face during an interview – "What was your last boss like?" or "Why did you resign from your last job?" Be positive in your approach. Even if you feel strongly against the last boss, don't make interviewers feel that you have such negative feelings against him. Rather, instead of talking about negative traits or behaviour, speak about what you learned from him in your personal and professional capacity. If you can't make out the positive points, don't speak negative either. Once a person starts speaking negative about someone, he is bound to look desperate and is likely to speak about torments he has faced at the hands of his last boss.

How You Fit The Job?

As we have discussed earlier, the intention of such a question is how you are better than others like a customer is likely to ask a salesperson about the stronger points of a commodity over that of a competitor's. What you are expected to do is to highlight your strong points – academic as well as personal, to make a favourable argument for yourself vis-à-vis the company. This is a vital question, as it would considerably influence the interviewers about your utility and ability. So, be prudent to choose the right words for the right occasion.

Where You Want To Be 10 Years From Now?

This is a tricky question that needs a prudent arrangement of words and opinions about yourself Don't try to play smart. You would make a fool of yourself. Be realistic in keeping with the post you have applied for, the opportunities the company provides for advancement, your ability and capacity to advance further, the role you wish to play in the organisation, and the methods you would like to adopt towards your and the organisation's advancement. And be cautious not to limit your ambitions in terms of the salary package, designation, etc. They are by-products of good performance, which have realistic value. Don't boast.

What Your Ideal Boss Would Be Like?

If asked, "When confronted with a lion what would you do?" "Nothing, it would be the lion". You cannot choose your boss; it is something one has to put up with. Here, don't go for personal likes and dislikes, but tell what qualities a team leader should possess, and how you can help him achieve organisational goals and objectives.

Questions On Inconsistencies

There is much likelihood of an interviewee being quizzed upon any inconsistency observed in the CV or his answers. Generally, it includes such questions as, "You are an LLB. What makes you opt for this and why don't you think about becoming an advocate?" These queries are aimed at your ability to synthesise your additional qualifications. Show your keen desire to make use of your additional qualifications in the post you have applied for in an advantageous manner.

Any Questions

Towards the end of an interview, there is a question that is generally asked, "Would you like to ask us a question?" Don't say "No". It would show your indifferent attitude and your lack of confidence of being selected and it would put your keenness to be a part of the organisation in jeopardy. Also, don't ask a question about the organisation that you are supposed to know from other sources before having reached the stage of the interview. Ask a question that would elicit your keenness to join the organisation. Asking a question like "What would be my target for the first year?" serves the dual purpose of impressing the interviewer with your desire to join the organisation and still remain in the seat of the aspirant.

Some Tips

> * Be accurate * Be brief * Be clear * Be consistent
> * Be polite * Be intimate but not friendly

While answering questions choose right words, prioritise your options and answer. Do not be swayed by the first or the last question, if the questions have come in the form of a rapid fire round. If need be, don't restrict yourself within the realm of the question and go well beyond the question to clarify a thought or process.

- *Be accurate in your answer.* Reply to what you have been asked. Don't explore the world you have not been asked to.
- *Be brief in your answers.* Don't camouflage your answers in verbose description.
- *Be clear.* Don't sacrifice clarity for the sake of being concise. There should be logic behind all your answers. All your deductions should be straight and simple as far as possible and should be well reasoned out.
- *Be consistent.* Don't contradict any of your statements given at any stage of the interview.
- *Be polite* and firm as to your ideologies.
- *Be intimate* but not friendly in your approach.

THE RIGHT APPROACH

A Psychological Approach

As has been repeatedly stated, an interview is an interactive process, which facilitates an interviewer to evaluate interpersonal attributes and communication skills of an individual and to assess his understanding of a wide variety of personal, social, technological issues, besides his desires and ambitions.

An interview is completely an unpredictable process where events can take any turn in which the interviewee has minimum chance of influencing the questions. However, with training and practice, a person can somewhat succeed in prompting an interviewer to ask such questions which would have a positive bearing on the outcome of the interview. It may be understood that an interview is a two-way process rather than a one-way questioning. If an interviewee is attempting to sell himself, it is also the organisation, which is selling itself. So, don't underestimate yourself, though the position of an interviewee cannot be counted on parallel terms with that of an interviewer.

An interviewer is not trying to locate a 'know all' person but is simply trying to find a suitable person who would fit the post in the best possible way and be helpful in accomplishing the organisation's targets, both short-term and long-term.

The Right Approach

The interviewer notes every activity which an interviewee undertakes, be it behaviour, attitude, the manner of answering questions, manners, speech, endurance to bear strains, etc. It is always advisable to shun such expressions, which may be in vogue in the form of slang's but are not part of the standard language.

Don't mix languages. Answer in the language you are confident in. Be it Hindi, English or a regional language, you should be able to express explicitly. And of course, the interviewer should also be able to understand the language.

Generally, interviewers are helpful and encouraging if the first impression is right and they try to help the candidate maintain his cool. But, be cautious. Sometimes, an interviewer tends to be helpful in a conceited manner by prompting the interviewee to fall in line and exposes his shortcomings to listen and believe what he hears and says. Wherever such a situation arises, be prudent to say, "You are right Sir, but I beg to differ."

Don't guess while answering questions. If you do not know an answer, admit your ignorance honestly. Don't try to cheat interviewers. They are more knowledgeable and have the ability to identify any such attempt.

An interview is more of a personality test rather than a grueling quizzing process. Interviewers are trying to find personal traits such as honesty, integrity, mental alertness, acumen, and ability to cope with different situations, your views on varied topics, general awareness and most importantly, your suitability for the job.

Anticipate questions and prepare answers and go on discussing them with friends and peers in a rational and logical manner. Try to support your deductions on the basis of data whenever necessary.

Do not get nervous before the interviewers. Be confident and have faith in yourself. It happens that most intelligent people fail to succeed, whereas people with far inferior knowledge succeed.

Put all your thoughts in a compact manner in your mind before you take a step to march towards the interview room.

Your Body Language

While entering the interview room adopt a relaxed, confident and motivated style or body language. In order to be relaxed, sit comfortably (keeping in mind, only when you are asked by the interview board member) and relax your shoulders. Raised shoulders restrict airflow and can cause the voice to be staccato. For women, legs should be uncrossed and kept together, with hands placed on the lap. This avoids the temptation to fidget, an obvious sign of nervousness. For men, legs can be crossed or uncrossed. If you do cross your legs though, cross them at the ankles, as it is unattractive and putting off for the interviewer to be facing a hairy lower leg. With the legs crossed at the ankle it can be helpful to squeeze them together if the pressure of the interview increases. This avoids adopting a defensive body language, such as folding the arms, leaning back in the chair, reducing eye contact and withdrawing from the conversation. Perhaps consider adopting a non-threatening 'query' expression, with the head on one side, a slight frown and a half-smile. It signals that you want to know more, but more importantly, that you haven't taken offence at what the interviewer has said. You should also turn your face towards the member who has asked you the question and should reply facing him.

Interviewers are human too and want to be appreciated and be comfortable with you. So, a final key to successful body language is to be aware of the interviewer's non-verbal signals. These are clues to your possible acceptance or rejection. You will know it when you are doing well if the interviewer is interested in what you have to say – reflected by leaning forward, smiling, nodding and maintaining a friendly eye contact. So take clues from the interviewer and copy their body language (subtly, of course).

If the interview isn't going too well, the non-verbal signals will be less positive such as leaning back from the desk, shaking the head, tapping fingers on the desk and avoiding eye contact. If you spot these signals, change your body language quickly and in any way you can. Talk more or talk less, smile more or less or use hands more or less. In short, do the opposite of what you've been doing so far. Accept that it may be too late to retrieve the situation, but nothing is lost by experimentation. It might help to tip the balance in your favour.

Lastly, it is crucial to be fully awake for your interview, especially if it's a late appointment. Increase your energy before the interview by jumping up and down in private for a few minutes. Raising one's heart beat slightly increases motivation. Alternatively, if it is impossible to do the jig, wake yourself up by dabbing cold water on your wrists and on the back of your neck to increase the blood flow.

Thus, signal throughout the interview that you will fit in with this company and, above all, be on your best behaviour.

The Wrong Approach

We have been discussing and insisting on several traits and manners to answer a question. In this chapter, we shall specifically deal with actual situation questions and answers that are wrong in approach but may or may not be factually wrong.

Let us understand that interviewers generally, summarily reject an interviewee who shows certain negative characteristics or basic defects. Conversely, interviewers take more time in assessing a candidate who may prove to be acceptable so that he could be put on the merit list. Answers to questions and queries have important bearing on the final outcome, and one should be cautious and prudent while answering them. While it is very easy to tell the approach of a certain person in total or that a particular answer is not up to the mark, but simply stating that a person is lacking also does not suffice. Here, we shall make an attempt to analyze various answers, which are factually correct but wrong in the approach. The areas generally probed by the board are (1) mental or intellectual (2) sociability (3) leadership qualities (4) organisational capacity and (5) personal.

Interviewers generally make a common list in accordance with the traits they look for in the candidate, and generally base their questions on such traits or to bring out such traits. This common approach is adopted to evaluate numerous candidates objectively without being prejudiced to any one candidate.

It is pertinent to note that different candidates would answer the same question in very many ways in accordance with the intellectual and other traits they possess.

An important point to be noted is that, the answers to questions should be brief, but not so brief as to mar clarity. Secondly, a candidate should try to expose his positive traits which otherwise may or may not be asked. So, a candidate must avail of every opportunity to bring out his traits stealthily. Revealing such extra traits helps the candidate most in the field he may be well-versed with.

Here, we shall discuss some questions and their answers in the wrong perspective and analyze as to what mistake has been committed by the candidate. This is being given to clarify to the various aspirants, to be explicit in their approach while answering a question.

Question: You had NCC training as mentioned in your application. Is it really beneficial to a person?

Answer: Yes Sir, it is very beneficial.

Analysis: The question was asked to put the candidate at ease and open up to the conversation. But with a limited answer, the candidate lost a good chance to show his knowledge and other traits, which could have been very beneficial for the outcome of the interview. His answer should have been:

"NCC training is basically military training imparted to students to inculcate various traits which are necessary for the development of a person in his personal capacity and to the society as a whole as it emphasises a lot on team work, proper planning, coordination, contingency plans, and organising things in entirety with objectives in mind. NCC training teaches a person not to leave anything to chance and teaches to synthesise and anticipate situations that may be eventual. This art of proper planning and organisation leads a person to become confident in his day to day work. Team work, cooperation and appreciation of other's responsibility coupled with tough physical training is bound to reflect upon one's personality in developing vital traits which are an asset for a lifetime."

Question: Should students be allowed to take active part in politics?

Answer: Students should be allowed to take part in politics as it is necessary for the healthy growth of our polity, but it spoils vital study hours, which can cause tremendous harm to the country.

Analysis: The candidate here is giving two contradicting statements in which he supports the view and gives a reason; but in the same breath refutes his stand counting on another demerit. The candidate seems to be perplexed as to the final answer. He should have taken a stand that it would have solved the shortcomings of the system. Going by the limited answer he gave, he should have paraphrased his answer as follows:

> "The knowledge of politics to the students is vital as it is necessary for the healthy growth of our polity and proves to be a fundamental concept. But since taking part in active politics also kills many vital study hours which have tremendous adverse impact upon the nation, the best way out is to impart the knowledge of polities to students so that healthy growth of our polity is ensured and at the same time, disallow active participation in

politics to alleviate any possibilities of loss of vital study hours which are equally crucial for the development of the nation as a whole."

Question: There is a recent trend that many students with technical, engineering, and computer backgrounds are entering into administrative fields, like civil services. How do you view it?

Answer: Candidates with technical, engineering and computer backgrounds have sharp minds and can contribute to the administrative field effectively with their technical know-how and focused approach. They should prove to be an asset to the field of administration.

Analysis: The candidate has done well to bring out certain innate qualities of technical personnel, but his answer is still incomplete, as he simply forgets about other fallouts – that is, the field that the students were trained for a particular purpose does not allow them to enter the field where they could have made better contributions. His answer rather should have been:

"The entry of technocrats into the administration is welcome for their sharp and focused approach when they learn while training for their respective fields. But the doubts are that all the resources spent on their education and training which are so scarce in our country, have gone waste. If at all these candidates dreamt of entering administration, they should have rather opted for humanities than going for technical know-how. Moreover, an administrator is more to do with managing things and knowing where from and how to get things done, than he himself being a technocrat. Moreover, moderate knowledge of computers and such technical fields is not the only preserve of these technocrats. It would be better, had these technocrats contributed to the country's growth by entering their respective fields of specialisation."

Question: During the reign of Indira Gandhi, countries of the world sought India's good offices to contain trouble spots in Asia, Africa and elsewhere. How have things changed that India does not count much in the world today?

Answer: Indira Gandhi was a lady who ruled the country iron-handedly and made her presence known to the world by all means – even if she had to use subtle means. Moreover, India's size and military might made other countries respect her. But today's political instability is the main reason why there is not much count for things to be in India's favour. Hence, India's declining influence in the world.

Analysis: The candidate is trying to give a false image of India as a country, which influenced the world with her military might. He has missed out on many important socio-political changes the world over, which he should have taken into consideration to give an answer. Moreover, the facts he has given are biased. India still remains a military power with the ability to influence the world opinion, since India's size remains the same. Though political instability seems to be there, yet it is one of the strengths of the country because change of power has always been smooth. Rather, his answer should have been:

"During the reign of Indira Gandhi, there was a state of Cold War in which two main countries of the world—the US and USSR played lead roles and who wanted to run the world as they wished. In this era, India took a lead role in representing those countries which wanted to be free from the influence of the two giants—the US and USSR, by being a founding member of NAM. Moreover, India being a large-sized developing country with growing economy was playing an important role while super powers opposed each other. After the Cold War ended, the world became a unipolar world with the disintegration of the USSR. Secondly, at present India is beset with growing internal problems such as terrorism and insurgency besides facing political instability in the absence of confident opposition. All these situations have led to the decline in India's stand as foreign countries do not wish to make long-term commitments and take risks."

Question: What would you do if you do not secure this job?

Answer: I shall try again and again with redoubled efforts to make certain that I secure this job.

Question: But the vacancies in this job are limited and it is unlikely to be advertised again in the near future.

Answer: Then Sir, I shall have to think again over my preferences.

Analysis: The candidate does not seem to have done his homework well. He is not aware of the number of posts in the organisation, nor is he aware of the ground vacancies in the near future. He also lacks in making alternative plans. The answer should have been such as would present the whole scenario. It is a must for all candidates to do their homework of acquiring knowledge about the organisation, the post, number of vacancies, and other related aspects, besides preparing for the worst, in case of a contingency that is not securing a job. Any wrong answer is likely to be probed further to bring out the real standing and preparedness of a candidate and it is thus important to review all situations beforehand than to grope in the dark.

Question: Has India done the correct thing in carrying out the second nuclear explosions at Pokhran?

Answer: Assuming that nuclear explosions were necessary for the security of the country, it was a good attempt—the earlier the better. We were prepared to do nuclear tests even earlier but such attempts failed due to international pressures and American threats. The present Vajpayee government has taken the plunge and has done what is essential for our national security.

Question: But with Pakistan following suit, India has lost the advantage. Isn't it!

Answer: Yes Sir, that's true.

Analysis: Interviewers generally lay a trap for candidates by asking a lead question wherein weak candidates are likely to say a simple "Yes" or "No" to such questions. Generally, such questions, as the second question

The Right Approach 83

above, are asked to put the candidate off the track, who is otherwise sailing smooth. And here, the candidate unknowingly, got trapped in the question by saying a simple "Yes". Although his answer to the first question was quite right, the second question was intended to prove his intellectual standard of meeting newer situations, where this candidate pitiably failed. His answer to the second question should have been thus:

> "You are right Sir, that India lost the initial advantage of entering the select nuclear club by the Pakistan explosions, but conducting such nuclear tests at such a short notice proves that either the tests were carried out by the Chinese or Americans on the Pakistan soil or it proves India's stand that Pakistan possessed nuclear weapons and was running a secret nuclear programme. Our explosions have done a great job in bringing out this fact in the open. Secondly, India with her vast resources can cope with international sanctions, which is quite impossible for Pakistan to endure and would result in adverse impact upon its economy."

(a) **Question:** You mentioned in your curriculum vitae that you are fond of seeing films. Is it?
   Answer: Yes Sir.
(b) **Question:** How often do you go to see films?
   Answer: Once a month.
(c) **Question:** I thought you go to see films at least once a week, if not more.
   Answer: Actually, Sir... (Keeps silent.)
(d) **Question:** Which film did you see last?
   Answer: It was xyz.
(e) **Question:** Who played the lead roles in xyz?
   Answer: It was Shahrukh and ... , I forgot the heroine.
(f) **Question:** Which was the best song of the film?
   Answer: All songs were good.

(g) Question: Did the film win any award?
Answer: I don't know, Sir.

(h) Question: Who is your favourite actor?
Answer: None

(i) Question: Who do you consider the best actor in Hindi Movies?
Answer: I can't say, Sir.

(j) Question: How do you go to see a film?
Answer: I just go by myself. If I get the ticket, I enter the hall, else I come back.

(k) Question: Do you know what Oscar award is?
Answer: Yes, Sir.

(l) Question: Has any Indian actor or film won it?
Answer: I don't know.

Analysis: The candidate has faired very poorly. He seems to have casually mentioned in his biodata that he is fond of seeing films whereas, in fact, he knows next to nothing about films, and this has created an adverse impact upon the interviewer. The rapid fire questions that followed were meant to probe the candidate as to his depth of knowledge, which proved to be quite superficial and untruthful. In the first place, the candidate should not have mentioned his interest in films. If at all he had, he should have endeavoured to gain some knowledge about this field because there is much likelihood of being posed questions on the information one supplies in his application or CV. Also, a candidate should grasp the opportunity of such questions to bring out some other positive traits in a bid to create a positive impression upon the interviewer and avoid rapid fire questions that may ensue. In response to the first question, the candidate simply said, "Yes". Compare his answer with the following answer:

> "Yes Sir, I like seeing films, particularly those recommended by my friends and frequency of such films is not more than once a month. I also like to see those films which have been appreciated by critics in newspapers and magazines."

The Right Approach 85

Just see how many positive traits have been brought out by the candidate in the answer to a single and not so important question. He has shown that he is social and has many friends who discuss latest developments in the society. He has clarified that though he is fond of seeing films, he does not waste time in seeing all those movies, which come his way. He is very selective. He has also brought out his interest in reading newspapers and magazines. And above all, he has saved himself the trouble of facing a volley of many further questions.

In answer to the second question (b) he has in fact belied the hope of the interviewer. He faltered in answering question (c). In answering question (j) he does show his lack of judgment, that he is not able to choose the best. In answers to the questions (g), (h), (i) he displays his indifference to his own very interest. While answering the question (j) he explicitly displays that he is not a social being; also, he has no contingency plan or pre-plans in case the situation of not getting tickets arise. Further in questions (k) and (l) he displays his little knowledge on the subject.

In total, the candidate has put himself in the dock and created such an adverse impression upon the interviewer that his selection for the post is unlikely.

Some Suggested Questions for Academic Interviews

Questions to Test Your Knowledge or Habits

What is the latest book you read? Prose, poetry, and fiction, historical ... ? Did you read it through? How would you summarise it in two minutes? What did you learn from it? Why did you choose this author? Why this book? Would you recommend this book to others? Why? On an average, how many books do you read in a year? What type? What are your favourite magazines? What are your favourite newspapers?

Did you read today's newspaper? Which one was it? What were the main headlines? What was the editorial theme? What do you read first in a newspaper? What last? Which part do you like most? Why? What do you think of the advertisement? How often do you read them? Which newspaper do you like best? Why? Do you read it daily?

Have yon read anything about Mahatma Gandhi? What books? What impresses you most about his life? From his teachings? From his actions? What do you think is Gandhi's main philosophies? What do you think is his major contribution to India? To the world? Which other Indian leader does come close to him? With whom would you identify him most - among philosophers? Among political leaders? Among emancipators? Among radicals? Among sages and saints?

Questions to Test Your Personality and Attitudes

Who has been the greatest influence in your life? Father? Grandfather? Mother? Grandmother? Brother? Sister? Friend? Enemy? Teacher? Boss? Classmate? What makes you think so? What were the major values you derived from this person? How do they affect your life? If you were to be the greatest person in someone else's life, what would be the greatest contribution you would make to that person's life? What makes you think so?

What is your idea of a manager? Who is an Indian manager? What type of a manager would you like to be? Why? How? As a manager-to-be, what are your major managerial assets and abilities? What is the role of a manager in India today? In the private sector? In the public sector? In the government? A manager is born, not made: Do you agree? What do you think are the ideal qualities of a manager? How do you plan to succeed in being an effective, successful manager?

Do you have many friends? How do you choose your friends? What is the criterion of a good friend? What do you normally expect from your best friend(s)? Companionship?

The Right Approach

Guidance? Leadership? Ideology? Honesty? Integrity? What do you think is your best contribution to your friends? Do you have many enemies? A friend gives, shares, and cares; do you agree? Are your best friends your age? Why? Do you feel comfortable with girl-friends?

What are your personal thoughts about the following?
(a) Massive urbanisation of villages
(b) Ruralisation of overcrowded cities
(c) Westernisation
(d) Rapid industrialisation
(e) Importing most recent technologies
(f) Nationwide family planning
(g) Nationalisation of all food industries
(h) Compulsory education up to grade-X for all
(i) Sex education in schools
(j) Students' participation in college unions

Questions to Test Your Social Awareness

What is the major problem in the world today? Oil crisis? Zionism? Neutron bomb? Communism? Socialism? Capitalism? Imbalance of power? Nuclear threat? Why? What are the social implications of these problems?

What are the major solutions to these problems? Who do you think creates these problems? How do they normally arise? How do they cease to be problems?

What is the major problem in India today? Poverty? Starvation? Unequal distribution of wealth, income and opportunities? Caste-system? Linguistic divisions? Religious differences? Political bankruptcy? As a manager-to-be how do you visualise your role in appraising and resolving these problems? How strongly do you feel about these problems and your responsibility for their resolution? Why?

Is there too much social injustice in the world today? Do you agree? What type of social injustice is this? What is the cause? What are the effects? What can be done about it?

Which country do you think is striving most to eradicate social injustices? Why do you think so? How deeply are these social injustices institutionalised and insurmountable? Why? What is the best form of government to eliminate social injustices? Why?

What do you think is the greatest social injustice in India today? Why? As a manager-to-be what would you do to rectify this situation? What do you think is the major source of crime, theft, poverty, malnutrition and inflation today in India? Why do you think so? What can you do about it?'

What would you consider is your greatest asset or achievement? Why do you think so? What are its implications to you, to your family, to your society, your country? How do your peers rate this asset or achievement? Do they agree to its significance both, for your life and for that of others?

What were the major factors that led to this asset or achievement? How much role and credit do you attribute to others in your present status?

Needless to say, these questions are neither exhaustive nor mutually exclusive.

They are, however, provocative and self-indicative. Much is left to the ingenuity of the interviewer to lead the interviewees to spontaneous character-revealing responses.

6

PRE-INTERVIEW GUIDELINES

Final Pre-Interview Checklist

> * Check Time and date of interview *Aware of your attitude and state of mind * Prepare expected topics * Prepared for different questioning styles * Plan outfit and route * Copy of your CV * Phone card and change * Research background of the company * Questions you would want to ask * Action mode

- Check the interview time and date. It is not uncommon for interviewees to misread the letter, so take another look.
- Are you aware of your attitude and/or state of mind? Get in the right frame of mind and ensure you portray your best side.
- Have you prepared the topics that are likely to crop-up? Do any last-minute preparation now.
- Are you aware of the different types of questioning styles?
- Plan your outfit and route.
- Have you got a copy of your CV or application form with you? Read through the forms one last time to remind yourself of the content and emphasis.

- Have you got a phone card and change with you in case you run late?
- Have you done your homework on the background of the company?
- Do you have some questions you want to ask?
- You are now ready for action—good luck!

Useful Hints For The Candidate

1. The members of the interview board will be watching the candidate carefully. Therefore, there should be nothing untoward in the manner of his entering the room. He should walk to his chair quite normally. There should be a natural soft smile on his face and his gait should be dignified.
2. Enter the room neither very hurriedly nor very slowly. Normal pace and dignified entry will characterise the candidate's appearance before the interview board.
3. Do not enter the room with a bowed head or a tense face.
4. The generally accepted manner of salutation is a simple good morning Sir or 'namaskar'.
5. Do not take your seat unless you are asked to do so. It is a mark of disrespect to the interviewers if you take your seat by yourself without being asked to do so. While taking your seat don't forget to thank the chairman.
6. Your manner of sitting before the interview board is also very important. You must remember that you are not sitting in your drawing room with your friends. Neither lean back on the chair nor sit stiff-necked. Be quite normal. After taking your seat, you should give a pleasant look at the chairman and wait patiently for him to speak.

Pre-interview Guidelines

7. Do not stand up when you are asked to answer a question. You should reply to the questions sitting calm.
8. You should not place your portfolio, containing your testimonials, etc., on the table. You should keep it down by your side.
9. Instead of keeping your hands under the table or on the table you should place them on the armrests in a normal position.
10. Speak in a soft but very clear tone. Your words should be well-chosen. They should convey your ideas clearly and unambiguously to the interviewers. Never speak in an affected tone or style. Your voice must not be hoarse or loud. Maintain normal pitch and normal speed.
11. Your manner of leaving the room is also of great importance. Do not get up before you are asked to do so. When you are told, "That will do, Mr ... ," you should get up from your seat without pushing the chair. You should politely thank the chairman, turn back and leave the room without looking back at the members while approaching the exit.
12. Try to show your interest in the job and never give the impression that you are casual.

Not To Forget

Remember the following rules of the game:

Study The Copy of Your Resume

Remember what you wrote under the column titles, "Why I wish to choose a career in management?" or "Your remarkable experience?" Most of the students tend to write these columns in a pretentious manner using description terms like innovative management, social responsibility, creativity, etc. Then, you better be sure you know what they mean. Someone is going to ask you what exactly you meant when you wrote them. Go through each word, each phrase you wrote, to make sure that you know their correct implication.

Try To "Lead" The Interviewer

The only way in which a rapport could be established between you and the interviewers is by means of your conversation. An interview is a two-way process. Yet a surprisingly large number of interviewees show a clear tendency to dodge the questions, some with a series of "Don't know", and others by giving half-hearted and inadequate answers. In most cases again, it is not ignorance, it seems to be more of a case of a nervous impulse, which makes the candidate concentrate on ending the interview as quickly as possible. He keeps hoping that fewer the questions the better, and that the sooner the 'whole damn thing' ends, the safer he is. If you get into this frame of mind, no interviewer, however considerate, can help you. Your mind goes blank as it were. You may have read the morning newspaper with a particular intention to remember the main headlines of the day. But when the question is asked, they escape your memory.

A tactful interviewee, on the other hand is relaxed. He has learnt the art of leading the interview. When a question is asked, he quickly searches his mind for an answer, which will "lead" the interviewer to ask him further questions, which he can confidently answer. Thus, when he is asked about the favourite subject, he will not merely say "economics" or "accounts". His answer, more likely will be, "economics, particularly international trade" or "accounts, particularly partnership accounts". He narrows down the scope of a question to a specific area in which he is good. By doing this he indirectly invites the examiner to ask him more questions in that area and thus, succeeds in providing a platform for the beginning of a pleasant conversation and a successful interview.

Be Your Natural Self

Do not put on artificial manners or accent or be rigidly formal. When you are asked your name, don't begin with the school boy fashion, "My name is ... (Just tell your name), "Prashant Gupta", "Piyush Chandra" or "Rajeev Krishna" and without adding "Mr" or "Miss". Interviewers can identify your sexual status all right.

Artificial manners which some put on for the occasion, just as they do for a new pair of shoes or a tie, draw attention towards themselves and can lead to awkward situations. There is a story about a candidate who entered the interviewer's room with a loud and courtly manner, "May I come in Sir". On entering the room, for a couple of seconds, when nobody asked him to sit, he ventured once again, "May I take your seat, Sir". Avoid such mishaps; they are caused by your being stiffly formal and bent on showing your elaborate good manners, which you have probably acquired just recently. For people used to being habitually polite, seldom say the complete sentence. It is just, "May I?" while asking permission to enter or to take a seat.

Avoiding stiff formality does not mean you should forget your politeness and lounge on the chair, use slang's or start fiddling with any object lying on the interviewers' table. Be relaxed, be yourself and be natural.

Exaggeration, Bluffing and Boasting

By all means, draw attention to your achievements (if any) politely at appropriate moments, but do not boast or exaggerate. Bluffing is a bigger crime; still, it is surprisingly common. Sample pieces of conversation are as follows:

"What do you do in your spare time?"

"I read. I am interested in books on Management."

"Which one of them did you read recently?"

"My Years with General Motors."

"But that's not a book on management. Could you mention a title you read on management?"

"I ... I can't remember"

Consider another example:

"Who's your favourite author?"

"Tolstoy"

"Which of his books have you read?"

"How Much Land Does A Man Require?"

"Well, can you tell me who wrote 'War and Peace' or 'Anna Karenina'?"

"I don't know."

"Have you read any book of *Chetan Bhagat*?"

"Yes Sir."

Have you read his book "*One Night @ The Call Centre?*"

"Perhaps, yes Sir."

"Do you know the name of the Hindi film based on this book?"

"Yes Sir, it was *'Hello'*."

The moral:

At an interview, you simply can't get away with exaggeration or bluffing. The candidate in the latter example above was not bluffing. He was simply exaggerating, perhaps, unintentionally. Once upon a time he had read a story written by *Tolstoy*. But he didn't know that the piece comprised a very unimportant contribution of *Tolstoy* to literature.

Listen More Talk Less

Listen attentively even when the interviewers are discussing some point, apparently, among themselves and talk only when you are asked to. Do not indulge in light-hearted small-talk, and don't be under the impression that by talking more, you can make an impression on them. Remember what the poet said:

Pre-interview Guidelines

'Words are like leaves and where they most abound. Much fruit of sense beneath is rarely found'.

Talk when talked to, explain adequately, but be discreetly brief.

Be a good listener. Listen and understand the question before attempting to answer it. If you have not understood it clearly kindly request the interviewer to repeat or clarify the question.

Some Do's and Don'ts

* Remember interviewers are experienced * Cover your weaknesses * Have confidence in yourself * Remain calm * Listen attentively * Be polite * Be energetic * Feel pleased * Develop your personality to suit the post * Be prompt * Establish a good rapport with interviewers * Be normal * Dress smartly * Be frank and honest

* Don't appear nervous * Don't speak in affected style * Don't elaborate answers* Don't interrupt interviewers * Don't argue * Request interviewer to repeat if a question is missed * Never answer until you have listened well * Do not hesitate in answering questions * Do not show ill manners * Do not be shabbily or gaudily dressed * Do not look gloomy * Do not talk more than needed * Do not boast * Do not try to evade answering questions * Do not be aggressive * Do not lose your presence of mind * Do not speak in a vague manner * Do not bluff or confuse the interviewer * Do not flatter the interviewer * Do not put counter questions * Do not hesitate to state the truth if you don't know the answers * Do not move unnecessarily

Do's

1. Remember that the interviewers are men of great experience. They are fully acquainted with the nature

of the duty and qualities required of a person for the particular job. They can judge a person's worth and his capabilities from his words and expression.

2. Give your best to the interviewers. Cover your weakness through the presentation of other achievements.
3. Have sufficient confidence in yourself to evoke confidence in the interviewers.
4. Remain unperturbed and composed and keep your interest throughout the interview.
5. First, listen very attentively and carefully to the question. Then answer it in a natural and normal way.
6. Adopt a pleasing manner of speech.
7. Follow the interviewers swiftly and adroitly and grasp the new question to tackle it with maximum energy and interest.
8. Feel pleased with your surroundings and be at ease in the company of the interviewers.
9. Develop your personality to suit the post for which you have applied.
10. Be prompt without being hasty, quick and aggressive and civil without cringing.
11. Establish a rapport with the interviewers.
12. Emit vivacity and enthusiasm from your looks and expressions.
13. Be perfectly normal.
14. Show pleasing and graceful manners, sufficient politeness and verve.
15. Be smartly and soberly dressed.
16. Gather adequate general knowledge before appearing at the interview.
17. Tell frankly if you are not able to answer any question or questions. In case the interviewer or interviewers suggest the answer, always show gratefulness to them by thanking them.

Pre-interview Guidelines

Don'ts

1. Do not appear nervous or shaky.
2. Do not speak in an affected style.
3. Do not try to elaborate your answer.
4. Do not interrupt the interviewer.
5. Do not enter into an argument with the interviewer.
6. If somehow, you miss a question you can request the interviewer to repeat it.
7. Never answer a question until you have listened to it well.
8. Do not hesitate in answering questions.
9. Do not show ill manners.
10. Do not be shabbily or gaudily dressed.
11. Do not look gloomy.
12. Do not talk more than what is needed.
13. Do not boast.
14. Do not try to evade answering the questions.
15. Do not be aggressive.
16. Do not lose your balance or presence of mind.
17. Do not speak in a vague or obscure manner.
18. Do not try to bluff or confuse the interviewer.
19. Do not try to flatter the interviewer.
20. Do not counter question.
21. Do not hesitate to show your ignorance, if you do not know the answer to a question.
22. Do not make unnecessary movements of any part of the body.

SAMPLE INTERVIEWS

Mock Interview No. 1

The Candidate

Prashant Agarwal is a candidate for an interview for the post of a manager in a firm. Presently, he is doing his MBA from Delhi University. We find him smartly dressed, well-groomed, and thus presenting an impressive first appearance. He is fairly tall, looks handsome with his athletic build and medium complexion and proves to be a ready mixer with his pleasant smile and friendly approach. He is wearing a dark suit of light material, which conforms to the formal occasion and fits him well. His grooming is impeccable, showing his taste and the importance he has given to the interview. At the reception desk he hands over the relevant documents and testimonials, completes all preliminary formalities and then goes to the waiting room, where he finds two lady candidates in one corner and one male candidate in another corner. Prashant prefers having a single group consisting of all the candidates and he decides to make the necessary efforts for that purpose. He decides to tackle the man first and walks towards him.

Prashant: Hello! Good Morning! I am Prashant Agarwal from Lucknow itself appearing for the interview. I believe you are also here for the same purpose (while walking he extends his hand for a handshake with Srikant). You look rather busy, reading the newspaper. Would it suit your convenience to have a chit-chat over a cup of tea or would you prefer to concentrate on the newspaper.

Srikant: Good Morning, Mr Prashant! You are most welcome.

I saw your name in the list displayed on the notice board. I had been waiting to meet you here rather early in the day You will be called for the interview before me. After me there is one S.D. Gupta, who is yet to arrive. The candidate, who was to be interviewed before you, was called inside only a couple of minutes back. He may take another 25 to 30 minutes. We can discuss our problems and have a friendly chit-chat in the meantime.

Prashant: Thank you, Mr Srikant. It is really a pleasure to meet you. I am afraid; I should not come in the way of your reading the newspaper. Naturally, you must be anxious to update yourself with the current affairs and burning topics of the day.

Srikant: Thank you, thank you, Prashant I have already read the newspaper. Since I was all alone here, I just started glancing through the newspaper all over again. Then those female candidates preferred to sit alone. Otherwise, I do not think that reading the newspaper at this stage would be of any help at the interview.

Prashant: Before proceeding with our talks, I would like those women candidates to join us, any objection to it. (Srikant nods). Okay (he walks up to women candidates). Would you please join us while we wait our turn for the interview? (Both women candidates join him). It may not be of immediate use, but knowledge never goes waste. Knowledge is power. Every news item, every article and every feature that we read, adds something to our knowledge, which may prove to be extremely useful at any stage in life, anywhere. At this interview itself, the Board might put some questions concerning the current trend in Indian politics. Look here. The newspaper is full of election-related news and articles. Who knows either or all of us may become politicians or the chief election commissioner at any stage in the distant future of our lives? In that case, the news and views read by us at this stage may illuminate our path when we need some light late in real life. Even otherwise, you can use the initiative and refer to it when the opportunity offers itself during the interview.

Shefali: This point is not clear to me. Why should interviewers be interested in our reading habits?

Prashant: Ms Shefali the interviewers have good reasons to find out our reading habits. They may like to find out how well informed you are about current national and international affairs and happenings around us. Your reading habits are indicative of the interest you display in the day-to-day problems. They may even put some questions regarding the progress made by India in various spheres including defence preparedness, nuclear science, and space research. They could also ask probing questions about the root cause of Kashmir problem and the cross-border terrorism, about the unstable political conditions in the country and the holding of frequent elections. They might also like to find out whether you find it necessary to carry out some electoral reform so as to ensure some stability and your views on the propriety of the actions of some political parties in causing the downfall of established governments without their ability to provide more stable alternative regimes. By and large, most of the topics, which come up for discussion during the interview, are those, which figure in the newspapers and periodicals.

Sneha: I didn't give much importance to it and I realise it to be my fallacy.

Srikant: (Interrupting): What is the real purpose of these interviews and personality tests? Do you think they are useful in finding our real self?

Prashant: (Smiling in a charming and cheerful manner) Well, it will require quite sometime for contemplating and discussing the answer to your question, in its proper perspective. First of all, we may have to consider what exactly are the personality traits or qualities of leadership required to be assessed or evaluated at this personality test or interview. I can briefly explain how interviewers can determine or come to some positive conclusions.

Shefali: It will be nice of you, Mr Prashant. Please elaborate this aspect. I think the real secret of success lies only in understanding this very approach.

Prashant: Perhaps you are right, Shefali. But I am only explaining this by way of illustration. I don't want any one of you to take my remarks personally or feel discouraged. Once we understand how our responses or answers to the questions at the interview in this specific instance will be interpreted, the whole thing will be resolved.

Sneha: Sure! We get your point. We don't think you are criticising any of us. Let us go ahead.

Prashant: One can assess the personality level of a candidate by talking to him just for half an hour or so. The types of questions the interviewers put to the candidate are general and more than one answer too, is probable. If the candidate deals with the subject on the basis of sound reasoning, he answers well, otherwise not. An interviewer is able to infer various personal traits from such answers.

Srikant: Thank you Mr Prashant, you have given us a lot of food for thought. Thank you very much for these valuable tips. Well, I think, they are calling you for the interview. There comes the messenger. We are sure you will come out with flying colours. Wish you the best of luck.

Prashant: Thanks to all the three of you. Wish you all the same. Bye. (He proceeds to the interview room with brisk and confident steps. At the entrance, he gently knocks on the door, seeks permission to enter, gently closes the door behind him and walks inside. He comes to a halt when close to the chair meant for the candidate, stands to attention and greets the chairman and members of the Board in a cheerful and audible manner. His bearing and approach make a favourable impression on the two interviewing members).

Interview

Prashant enters the Interview Room very confidently and with firm determination and a smiling face.

Prashant: Good Morning to you all, Sirs!

Interviewer: Good Morning, Mr Prashant. Please take your seat and be comfortable.

(Prashant Agarwal takes his seat on the chair meant for the candidate. He is well-organised and makes least noise. A smile is always playing on his bright face. He now looks up to the interviewer with expectation, for his further commands and waits in full readiness and with a keen interest to meet the barrage of questions, which are to follow).

Interviewer: Mr Prashant, I found from your curriculum vitae that you have studied political science at the university and gained second division in M.A. in the subject. Was it your intention to become a politician and enter into active politics?

Prashant: (Smiling) No, Sir. Not at all, neither then, nor now. I am not keen on becoming a politician. My goal has always been the administration and managing the affairs of a business house of a reputed house like yours. And I chose political science as one of my subjects of academic study as I felt it would help me to discharge my responsibilities effectively as an administrator in an organisation that I have dreamed of.

Interviewer: That is interesting. Can you explain how the study of Political Science can be helpful to a manager?

Prashant: Sir, the administrator or manager has to play a key role in implementing the plans of an organisation and other related programmes in the context of good performance. By studying political science, not only can we understand the working of our own constitution and institutions but also know how the work in other organisations can be managed in a suitable manner. Thus, I am convinced that the study of political science could be of great help to the administrators and managers.

Interviewer: Well, I agree you have something there although many who have not studied political science have also become excellent administrators, both in India and abroad. But tell me why do you not want to join active politics? Is it your view that educated youth should eschew active politics?

Prashant: No, Sir, not at all. I wonder whether I had conveyed such an impression. If so I am very sorry, indeed. I firmly believe that good education is a basic and fundamental requirement for all, no matter one's profession or vocation in life. It is all the more so in the case of politicians. Of course, it will also help if politicians had undergone the study of political science as an academic subject.

Interviewer: Then why are you not keen on joining active politics?

Prashant: (Smiling) Shall I say, Sir that it calls for a certain type of mental attitude, adjustability and adaptability to function and have a special interest and drive for active politics. Above all, politics is an expensive game and you need lots of money. May be I lack these and in any case, as I said earlier, my goal right from the beginning has been to make a career in administrative cadre and I deliberately did not allow myself to be led away from my chosen goal.

Interviewer: I suppose you are aware that the world, which, of course, includes our country, has seen many able politicians who did not have any formal university education. For example, one can cite some well-known film star politicians and many more.

Prashant: I beg your pardon, Sir. I referred to good education; if I remember correctly and not to formal university education and acquisition of degrees as such. The great Winston Churchill and Abraham Lincoln did not boast of master's degrees. But they acquired good education through their own efforts. The film star turned politicians, I would say, are exceptions to the rule. Even they could shine as still better politicians if they had university education.

Interviewer: You indirectly hinted at money power in politics. Can you say that we have successfully operated democracy in Independent India and that it has taken roots in this country?

Prashant: We can say that we are still retaining democracy in this land even after 61 years of Independence and in the face of much diversity, whereas it has fallen by the wayside in many other countries, which opted for democracy on attaining independence after World War II. That is a red letter achievement by itself. As for its taking roots here, I have my own doubts. I am inclined to agree with Dr Ambedkar who observed that democracy in India is nothing but a top dressing on alien soil. To have it deep-rooted, democracy will have to grow through evolution and people will have to be made used to it. They must have education and acquire a stake in preserving democratic institutions A citizen should know the value of his vote and exercise it judiciously and with care and caution. I am sorry to say that these factors are absent in our country. Since black money and corruption are rampant, it is doubtful whether democracy could survive their increasing onslaughts for long.

Comments: The interviewer starts the interview referring to the educational background of the candidate, who finds in him an opportunity and opening to communicate his keenness and planned approach to make the grade. He is also able to answer in-depth a question on the subject of his academic study. The candidate displays the courage of his convictions and also the tact and ability to disagree in an agreeable manner. He shows good awareness of his surroundings and also the role he can play as an administrator.

Interviewer: What is your assessment about the supply management concept in economics? How far has it proved successful in America and in India?

Sample Interviews

Prashant: The supply management theory in economics revolves round the control of money supply in the country's economy at any given time. According to its protagonists, by restricting the money supply, through the system of credit squeeze, inflation can be controlled, if not immediately, at least in the near future, say some eight to twelve months. By putting up the interest rates steeply and cutting out all welfare expenditure, the former US President Ronald Reagan had tried to bring down inflation and reduce unemployment ratio, but it had not worked well. Capital had become scarce and production had not picked up. The high interest rate got adversely affected and the value of dollar lost ground to other currencies. The unemployment ratio has also shot up. Thus, this approach had not shown positive results in the USA. In India also, the position remains the same. Lack of capital is hampering industrial growth and expansion. In addition, India had to import even items like sugar, edible oils, etc., leading to adverse balance of payments situation in foreign exchange reserves.

> **Comments:** The candidate explains a complex concept in a simple language with good understanding. He has the intellectual integrity to state the truth of his convictions, frankly and freely. His conclusions are supported by rational and logical arguments with reasons. The candidate can carry his men with him even under frying circumstances. He is bold and courageous and takes reasonable risks. He has no difficulty in making up his mind and arriving at firm decisions.

Interviewer: Why does India not command the influence in the international community warranted by its size and population?

Prashant: India is a developing country. In spite of it being one of the fastest emerging markets and militarily powerful countries, India is not given its due in the international fora. The West's adverse reaction against India's nuclear explosion is a case in point. With US diplomacy tilted towards Pakistan and China, India seldom found a favourite place in the US policy, though we have gained some ground in international relations against Pakistan after the Kargil War. Further, despite India's strong eligibility to become a permanent member of the United Nations Security Council, the opposition by the western countries gives ample evidence of a bias against India.

Interviewer: Both Japan and Germany are economically very strong, though militarily they are nowhere. Why despite their economic wealth, do they not have any military strength?

Prashant: Both Japan and Germany could gain economic superiority because they do not have to incur any military expenditure. The security of Japan and Germany is underwritten by America. Based on past experience, America and its western allies like the UK and France do not want Japan and Germany to enjoy any military clout.

Comments: The answer shows that the candidate has benefited from reading newspapers and magazines. This candidate has kept himself fully abreast of international developments and argues his case on the strength of knowledge, understanding and firm conviction. His views are mature and realistic. His arguments are fully supported by sound and logical reasoning. Once again, he does not hesitate to offer his original, honest and considered views for what they are worth. Thus, his intellectual integrity and mental courage stand confirmed and vindicated. He speaks out his mind frankly without fear or favour. Since his arguments are rational, logical and objective, he is able to convince and carry his listeners' along with him.

Interviewer: Well, how do you explain the contradiction between cricket matches and bus journeys on the one hand and the test of Agni, Ghauri and Shaheen on the other?

Prashant: As far as I can understand, there are a lot of people in both the countries who want peace and goodwill to prevail. They feel elated at cricket matches and bus journeys.

But in both the countries there are a large number of hawks too. The people at the helm of affairs in both the countries have now understood that in the event of a conflict, both the countries are liable to be destroyed lock, stock and barrel. Therefore, they want to improve relations. But both of them have to keep the hawks in their respective countries in good humour because these hawks can dislodge the people in power at the moment. Therefore, the people who want peace between our two countries have also to keep the Agnis, Ghauris and Shaheen testing from time to time to safeguard their chairs. It is really a strange situation. Unbelievable it may look, but it seems to be true.

Interviewer: Do you think that there is a real danger of a nuclear war between India and Pakistan?

Prashant: No Sir, the reason being that now both the countries possess nuclear weapons and long-range missiles. Both the countries know that there are no winners in a nuclear war. All are losers. Moreover, in case of a nuclear war between any two countries, the death and destruction is not restricted only to the belligerent nations, but the entire human race is likely to suffer immensely. Therefore, the chances of a nuclear war between the two countries are remote. The real danger is that Pakistan may pass on the nuclear technology to other Muslim countries and some terrorist groups. In that case, things may fall into irresponsible hands. Further, the danger of accidental explosions of nuclear weapons anywhere is fraught with serious consequences.

Comments: This again shows that the candidate has a keen and in-depth knowledge and understanding of the burning topics of the day. This understanding and keen intellect are sure to stand him in good stead, wherever he goes. Needless to say that the interviewer has been deeply impressed by his performance.

Interviewer: Do you think agricultural growth will create adequate employment opportunities to erase the existing problem of unemployment?

Prashant: Learning from the experience of industrialised and developed countries, this strategy may not be valid. Agricultural growth can take place by intensive cultivation, as in Japan, America and elsewhere. It can also take place by increasing the area under cultivation. For our Green Revolution, we experimented with both the methods and succeeded. But the scope of bringing more areas under cultivation is quite limited because of soil, terrain, water and climatic constraints. Thus, deserts, mountain ranges, stony plateaus, drought-prone regions, etc., cannot be easily brought under cultivation. Cost-wise too, it will not be a viable preposition. Hence, greater emphasis needs to be placed on intensive cultivation, which ultimately would simply mean large-scale mechanised farming. Thus, in the long-run, the scope for employment in agricultural activity would diminish and people will have to move from agriculture to industry and other allied professions with the adoption of Industrial Revolution. This has happened in the western countries and India will be no exception to this rule. In future, only greater industrial growth can solve the unemployment problem. We can successfully tackle both the food and unemployment problem, by controlling the population explosion. So long the present population growth continues all our efforts to end unemployment are not likely to succeed even with the investment of large amounts of work and finances.

Interviewer: Would you say that industrialisation in India has not progressed to the desired extent because of our preferential treatment to the public sector?

Prashant: The public sector has some decided advantages over free market and private industrialisation the most important facility being availability of capital. Through the government, banks, financial institutions and overseas resources, the public sector undertakings can easily obtain capital, land, machinery, technical collaboration, etc., necessary for production. The snag is in the area of productivity, economy, operational efficiency, etc. Since survival and service are guaranteed to the employees and they get innumerable concessions and legal protection, there is no motivation for their sincerely working. There is also no accountability. There exist usual evils of red tap, bureaucracy and delay in decision-making, though, there are exceptions and some public sector units are run quite efficiently. Also, one will concede that all private industries too are not being run efficiently. The best thing is to remove the monopoly and allow the public sector undertakings to compete with their counterparts in the private sector on equal footing. It will force the former to run on professional and efficient lines. Secondly, pampering of the inefficient, merely for the sake of votes, should stop. Industrial discipline should be enforced.

> **Comments:** The candidate displays keenness, urge, is enterprising and enthusiasm. He has paid adequate attention to his appearance, turnout and bearing to ensure the initial favourable impact. Next, he is found to be socially warm, friendly and a good mixer.
>
> He enjoys the company of others, cultivates new friends and shows interest and involvement in people. He proves to be enterprising, takes initiative, seeks out opportunities and accepts fair risks. He also enjoys good organising ability and power of expression. He comes out with his original ideas without fear or favour but makes sure they are rational and sound. His strong points can be summed up as social adaptability, self-confidence, sense of responsibility, cheerful disposition and fluency of expression.

Interviewer: As we have discussed earlier that India does not count much in the international relations and it has no role to play in the world arena. At one time the super powers sought India's good offices to contain trouble spots in Asia, Africa, and elsewhere. How do you account for India's decline at the world stage?

Prashant: India, as a founder-member of NAM and also as a large-size developing country with a growing economy, was playing an important role when the Super Powers were opposing each other and the Cold War was raging at its peak. Now the Cold War has ended. To that extent the NAM and its leader, India, have lost their importance. Secondly, the Soviet Union has disintegrated and America has emerged as the unipolar super power. Thirdly, India is beset with growing internal insurgency and terrorism. Lastly, we are also facing political uncertainties in the country. In this uncertain situation, foreign countries do not wish to take risks and make long-term commitments. All these, in my view, account for our relatively subdued role in international relations.

Interviewer: What lessons should India learn from the demise of the Soviet Union, which was once a Super Power?

Prashant: The Soviet Union attained the status of a Super Power under the ruthless dictatorship of Joseph Stalin. Its military might including its nuclear arsenal and missile force like ICBMs, etc., and space satellites was built at the cost of the country's industrial and economic development. After the death of Stalin, people wanted economic betterment and political freedom. M. Gorbachev brought in several reforms and introduced democracy and market economy. This sudden shift resulted in the disintegration of the Soviet Union. As for India, it started and remains as the world's largest democracy. We are changing over from mixed economy to free market economy in a phased manner. Thus, the situation between U.S.S.R. and India is different. We must ensure that our democracy is preserved. At the same time, we must have better rate of economic growth.

Interviewer: In recent years, despite a late start, countries like Singapore, Malaysia, Taiwan and South Korea have registered phenomenal economic growth. Whereas, India, which had nearly two decades of a head start over them, is sadly lagging behind. How could this be explained?

Prashant: (Smiling) It is difficult to compare India with these countries for a number of reasons. First and foremost, we should take note of India's chosen goals and objectives in the national and international spheres. Internally, it has opted for democratic socialism, a totally alien concept to the

India soil. Secondly, socialism and democracy cannot be easily reconciled. In the international sphere, we have embraced non-alignment as the cornerstone of our foreign policy and this has cost us a great deal. We could not get US economic aid to the extent and scale as obtained by South Korea, Taiwan, etc. Similarly, our socialist goal barred collaboration with multinational industrial giants as was done by Singapore, Malaysia, etc. Besides, Singapore and Malaysia are comparatively small countries with limited population. They have strong rightist or totally authoritarian regimes and do not practice universal adult franchise as we do in India. We have regional, linguistic and communal problems besides social, political and economic legacies. About 65 per cent of our 950 million people are illiterate. We have had three wars with Pakistan and one with China. There are free elections held at regular intervals. When we take all these aspects into account, it must be said that India has made reasonably good progress both economically and politically.

Comments: The candidate has shown comprehensive knowledge and shrewd understanding of the social, political and economic developments taking place in India and other countries. He is realistic and practical.

Interviewer: Do you think that India is justified in carrying out three nuclear explosion tests at Pokhran on May 11, 1998 and two more such tests further on May 13, 1998?

Prashant: Certainly Sir, India has got to safeguard its frontiers and it should not be vulnerable to nuclear threats from China and its proxy Pakistan in particular. Similarly, India should be able to stand up against nuclear blackmail of America, France and the U.K. As our former Prime Minister Mr A.B. Vajpayee declared, India should have conducted these tests long ago, especially after atmospheric nuclear tests were carried out by France and China in recent years.

Interviewer: Will not the economic and other aid or loan sanctions now being imposed by America and its allies, including Japan as a sequel to these atomic expositions adversely affect our economic growth?

Prashant: Yes Sir, it may have some adverse impact in the short-run. But in the long-run it will free us from leaning on foreign crutches. We will learn to stand, walk, march and run on our own legs. In the past, China, Vietnam, Soviet Union and Iraq have also faced more stringent sanctions of this kind. They have not only survived but also emerged stronger. Now, the industrialised West is running after them. We have a lot to learn from Vietnam who has taught lessons to not only the mighty US but also to the so-called giant China. The Americans are terribly scared of China and its Red Army. But the Vietnamese have beaten the Chinese and their Red Army without any outside help.

Interviewer: What is the basis of Left parties and some intellectuals criticising our present nuclear explosions?

Prashant: The Left parties who are totally brainwashed are mere mouthpieces of their Chinese masters and they cannot but echo their masters' voice. The self-styled intellectuals are aping their Western counterparts because of the glitter of American dollars.

Interviewer: Should India go ahead to produce nuclear weapons?

Prashant: Most certainly. Only then America and its allies will recognise India as a true nuclear power.

Interviewer: Don't you think it a better option to use our limited resources to improve the lot of India's poor than to produce nuclear weapons?

Prashant: National Security takes precedence over everything else. China has armed Pakistan with nuclear weapons and missiles and both China and America will make Pakistan attack India. It has happened in the past and future is not likely to be an exception to this. The first priority then for us is to survive as a nation and not allow ourselves to be disintegrated and enslaved yet again.

Interviewer: What about the lot of the poor?

Sample Interviews

Prashant: Sir, we are exploding nuclear devices after a quarter of a century. Since our first Pokhran explosion of May 1974, we have not diverted funds to nuclear weapons for nearly 34 years. Where have the resources gone? Has the lot of the poor improved? How have they benefited? We cannot dissolve our armed forces. We have to have a Defence budget to meet our security needs adequately and the nuclear weapons will be confined to the defence budget.

Comments: The interviewer probed the candidate at some length in the field of international relations. It is seen that the candidate is well-versed in this sphere and possesses extensive ideas. He is able to grasp the significance and real purpose of the questions and express opinions, which reflect imagination, proper appreciation and adequate originality. His knowledge is up-to-date and he has kept himself abreast of current developments. He has the courage to state his honest and considered views for what they are worth without any inhibitions or extraneous considerations. He is assertive as well as persuasive, takes firm decisions and stands by them with determination.

Interviewer: That will do, your interview is over. You can leave now Prashant.

Prashant: Thank you, Sir (He leaves the room gently but with confidence).

Final Outcome: It is obvious from the above proceedings that the candidate knows that an interview is not a mere question and answer session. He has offered his views unreservedly and freely on all questions posed to him. He did not stray away from the subject nor did he repeat himself. His performance confirms that he is well-read and intelligent. He understands and grasps the implications and the scope of the questions correctly and quickly. He readily perceives the pros and cons of a problem or situation in a realistic and imaginative way. One could readily gauge that he has an analytical mind,

> a rational approach and a logical way of reasoning. He is bold and full of courage and ready to meet new challenges, strike out new paths and shoulder new responsibilities. He is sure of himself and his enthusiasm is contagious. His ability to speak eloquently and present his ideas successfully is a real asset. His impact on the interviewers throughout has been forceful and favourable. A positive and optimistic candidate, Prashant Agarwal is a man of action who can be depended upon to accomplish the organisational goals and deliver the desired result by winning others to his way of thinking.

Mock Interview No. 2

The Candidate

Piyush Gupta is a lean built young man of good height about five feet and nine inches with medium whitish complexion. So far as physical attributes are concerned, he is just like any other average individual of his age, education and background. Nevertheless, he at once attracts attention because of his perpetual smile playing on his lips, liveliness, remarkable enthusiasm and unbounded vigour. His gait, walk, and other general movements indicate self-confidence. His eyes are full of life and reflect amiability, friendship, warmth, cordiality and genuine interest. He greets others, be they friends or strangers, be they members of the same sex or the opposite, in a pleasant, ringing voice and with a steady handshake or a graceful *namaste,* as appropriate. At the waiting room, he is fully at ease in the company of three other candidates, one of whom happens to be a lady. Although all the three were utter strangers to him till a few moments ago, now he is already on terms of addressing them by their first names. We find them all engaged in an interesting discussion and the subject naturally pertains to the interview at hand.

Nitin: Mr Piyush, you said that one can methodically prepare oneself for this personality test. Can you please tell us how exactly you have prepared yourself?

Piyush: Firstly, I prepared myself for the probable questions that could crop-up in the interview, like my educational background, extra-curricular activities, nature of my present job, why I wish to join this job, etc. I also gave a quick run-through to my optional subjects—social science and history. I drew up a list of expected questions and thought of convincing explanations for the same. I also consulted some seniors, who have been successful in this post in the recent past. I also had practiced interview sessions with my teacher in the college and with my brother at home. In addition, I have been regularly going through the observations of toppers in various examinations and the model 'live' interviews appearing each month in different books and magazines. Finally, of course, I have been reading publications like the Time India Today Yojana, NCERT books, NBT publications, India Year Book and Five-Year Plan document, besides the daily newspapers.

Poonam: How can one find the time to read so much?

Piyush: (Smiling again) Well, for one thing, I developed the reading habit right from my school days. All it requires is self-discipline and adhering to a strict schedule drawn up by yourself. You have to decide on your priorities and spend your time accordingly. The college authorities also were kind and helpful by granting me a month's leave and allowing me to use the college library and reading room freely.

Vasudewan: Do you think, Mr Piyush that the first impression counts more than anything else in the personality test or interview?

Piyush: I dare say, it helps, but it will not suffice. However, a definite negative first impact, especially in key personality traits like honesty, cooperation, adaptability, etc., may possess other merits like high intelligence, power of expression, decisiveness and so on.

Nitin: I agree honesty is a key factor. But how can the board find out whether a candidate is honest or not? They cannot ask direct questions and get direct, shall I say, 'honest' answers (he laughs and others join him).

Piyush: You are perfectly right, Mr Nitin. The board will not, and does not ask direct questions to find out the personality traits of the candidate in any sphere, whether it relates to character or other leadership factors. But such personality attributes are gauged and deduced from the answers given by the candidate and the attitude displayed by him during the interview. For example, if the board observes that the information furnished by a candidate about his hobbies and interests is incorrect in the context of the answers given by him during the interview, it would doubt his honesty. Honesty does not imply only not stealing, but also extends to truthfulness, sincerity, etc. In the same way, the social, dynamic and leadership qualities can be perceived and evaluated from his answer during the interview. Similarly, if a candidate repeatedly bluffs, instead of truthfully pleading his ignorance in certain matters, it could be construed as dishonesty.

Vasudewan: Thank you, Mr Piyush. Your clarifications are apt and very useful. I can see they are now summoning you for the interview. We all wish you the very best.

Piyush: Thank you and wish the same to you all.

(He takes leave of his friends. After obtaining permission, he enters the interview room and gracefully walks towards the chairperson and a member seated behind an oval desk).

Piyush: (Continuing to stand upright in a true army fashion) Good morning to you, Sir's.

Interviewer: Good morning to you, Mr Piyush. Please be seated.

Piyush: Thank you, Sir. (He sits on the chair indicated by the chairman. He remains relaxed and is smiling but attentive. There is no nervousness or visible anxiety on his part. He maintains cool and collected with a smile adorned on his lips).

Interviewer: I see you have undergone NCC training for five years. How did you like it?

Piyush: Very interesting, educative and useful, Sir. I thoroughly enjoyed it, especially the camp life, despite physical exertions and extra demand on our time, including holidays.

Interviewer: Sounds good to hear that. But there seems to be some contradiction in what you say. You said it was physically tough and cost your holidays too. Yet you found it enjoyable. How do you reconcile that?

Piyush: (Smiles) It was certainly tough and tiring, but it is also a fact that one can enjoy physical exertion by suitable training and habit. The health runs in the mornings, PT, parades, arms drill, long route march, crass-country, etc., all becomes enjoyable once we get used to them. It is all adventure, new experience and new knowledge. You have good company and you do it as a team. There is healthy competition. The camp fire is great fun. During college holidays and vacations we had NCC camps where actual army life was simulated to reality.

Interviewer: Did it not hinder your studies?

Piyush: No Sir, I was able to pay attention to my studios without any difficulty. However, I cannot say the same with regard to my sports activities. I could not concentrate and do justice to my favourite game of cricket for scarcity of time. I had to choose between NCC and cricket and I gave priority to NCC.

Interviewer: Was it not because of more discipline in NCC that you could not afford to be absent from parades, camps, etc?

Piyush: One has got to be equally disciplined in sports also if one is determined to achieve distinction. One has to keep exercising and do long hours of net practice. I felt that I could not get NCC training on my own while I could play cricket on my own. However, to become a top or national Test player in cricket, you have to concentrate and put in long hours of work. That is where I faced the problem. I had to choose between the two. With NCC, I could still keep in touch with sports and athletics. In fact, NCC encourages organised games a good deal. But if you decide to concentrate on sports you cannot tag along NCC. It won't be justice to NCC.

Interviewer: I agree with you. Nevertheless, with your special liking for NCC, you might have preferred a career with the defence forces to that with this administrative job.

Piyush: I suppose you are right, Sir, but I had to make up my mind to join this job right from the beginning. Looking back, one of the motivating factors to choose NCC over cricket was the fact that it would have proved difficult to gain military training later, as I had already decided to try for this job. In my view, an administrative officer with a military training background would be an asset to the organisation with the traits that result from such military training.

> **Comments:** The interviewer saw the candidate standing smartly and greeting the interview board. The records also showed that Mr Piyush had distinguished himself in the NCC with five years of training to his credit. Hence, he chose the topic as the starting point for the interview. However, the candidate used it as an opportunity to put across his strong points in a subtle manner. We could see that the candidate is proficient in studies, as well as in sports. He can decide on his priorities and make up his mind firmly. He plans well in advance and works according to the plan to attain his goal, mobilising and utilising his resources with intelligence and imagination. The NCC training has helped him to move closer towards his career goal.

Interviewer: Mr Piyush, how did you prepare yourself for this personality test or interview, provided, of course, if you did prepare at all?

Piyush: Yes Sir, I did prepare for this personality test, as I did for the preliminary and written tests. I am determined to make the grade of this post and accordingly, I went about the task in a planned and organised manner, putting my resources and time at my disposal to the best possible use. Basically, my preparations for the written papers and the interview are inter-linked. I made brief notes of whatever I had studied for the written examination. Particularly, I paid special attention on my optional subjects. I am a regular reader of The Hindustan Times and also of several periodicals like the Time, Newsweek, Observer, India Today, Competition Success Review, Times of India, Reader's Digest and the like. These periodicals helped me a lot, with their varied approach to different points of view and happenings in fields like general knowledge, current events and personality development. Further, I also sought guidance from some friends who had appeared for such interviews, whether in the IAS or other competitive examinations. Finally, I asked my brothers, one of whom is an IAS officer and another major in the army, to conduct several mock interview sessions with me. I also attended an institute for their training programme. For about two months, I read different newspapers published in India and abroad. I was especially interested in the editorial and special articles. Even with my friends, I made it a point to discuss, as much as possible, the burning events and topics. As I said at the beginning that I am keen and determined to successfully make the grade for this post.

> **Comments:** We find this candidate to be a well-motivated and dynamic individual. He has cultivated the right mental attitude, social behavioural manners to prove charming and remains endearing to others. He has no inhibitions and mixes freely with others. He is tactful, cooperative and very adaptable. He does not thrust himself on others, but wins them over by his helpful and endearing conduct. In the preliminary discussion with the interviewer, he got an opportunity to exercise his initiative and we see him utilising the opportunity to the fullest extent. Further, we get a picture of his favourable family background and the large circle of friends he enjoys. His relations with his elders and seniors are on excellent terms

and he has been able to enlist their support readily. He has a definite goal and works to achieve that goal. Thus, with his opening answer, this candidate has made a favourable and forceful impact on the interviewers.

Interviewer: The Indian constitution is progressive as far as the status of women in our country is concerned. There is no discrimination on grounds of sex. Would you say that the women in India are better off and fully emancipated?

Piyush: I agree with you totally, Sir, that our constitution has given equal rights to women. However, it is one thing to lay down the law and another to translate the law into reality. I cannot say that the lot of the women in India is a very happy one. By and large, the majority of women in India are dominated by men. Their lack of education, economic dependence, and also lack of knowledge and skills compel them to be totally dependent on the men folk. I feel that the women should be given due education and they should be enabled to acquire technical skills, so that they can gain economic independence. Once women are educated, skilled, and become economically self-reliant, they would be able to enjoy the rights conferred on them by the constitution.

Comments: The candidate has a good knowledge of current affairs. He is able to think and present his views coherently, intelligently and realistically. His ideas are original and his conclusions proceed on logical and rational lines. It is evident that he has assimilated what he has been reading. He can arrive at independent conclusions exercising good judgement and foresight.

Interviewer: Do you think that judicial activism as we have been seeing now is for the good of our democracy?

Piyush: There cannot be two opinions regarding this. An active judiciary ensures the protection of the rights of citizens. Through what is called Public Interest Litigation (PIL), it has been possible for any individual or an organisation to secure justice at the apex court of the country.

One cannot probably blame the court for taking up vital issues of concern and acting on them when they find the executive is moving at a snail's pace. Some of the issues taken up by the court like asking the hospitals to provide for a better layout to dispose of wastes or asking the corporations to keep the city clean, must be keeping the concerned on the alert. Apart from these issues the court has taken a stand on the burning issues of corruption like the notorious *hawala* case and the housing scam or the fodder scam in Bihar.

Interviewer: Well, how do you react to the Orissa Chief Minister exercising his right of vote as MP, which led to the toppling of the Vajpayee Government by just one vote in the no-confidence motion?

Piyush: Sir, I personally feel it was unethical on the part of Mr Giridhar Gamang to have participated in the voting. Having occupied the office of Orissa CM, he should not have exercised this right, without which the government could not have been toppled and we would have been spared of another election. Having voted as MP, he should have resigned as CM and should have reverted, as member, Lok Sabha. He didn't do this either.

> **Comments:** The candidate is well-versed with the current national and international events. He is able to express mature views and substantiate his arguments with proper rationale and logic. He is free and frank and speaks out his mind boldly without any inhibitions.

Interviewer: From your dossier, I find you have done M.A., B. Ed and presently you are a lecturer in a degree college. You have also registered yourself for PhD. Don't you feel that you might find this job dull and drab keeping in mind your academic interests and excellence?

Piyush: (Smiling) I have opted for the academic and teaching fields as a means to realise my ambition of making grade for this administrative post. My involvement with the academic subjects has helped me in my written examination.

Interviewer: Can you explain as you would do to a layman, what exactly deficit financing implies and how is it linked up with inflation?

Piyush: Deficit financing means increasing the amount of money in circulation at a given time, by printing and pumping in more paper currency by the government of a country, but there is no corresponding increase in the amount of goods produced. Since the supply of goods remains constant and that of money increases, naturally there is a rush for the restricted goods available in the market making the prices shoot up. But, if the increase in money supply were made with the intent to increase production, soon there would be more goods, greater employment and market expansion leading to economic growth. Thus, if increased money supply is directed towards non-productive expenditure, it will lead to inflation. If deficit financing is used to step up production of goods and services, it will result in good economic growth and higher per capita income.

Interviewer: What about price control and regulated distribution exercised by the government? Will they not help contain inflation?

Piyush: Price control and regulated distribution are temporary measures and are unlikely to succeed in the long-run. They will prove counter-productive under free economy and give rise to corruption, hoarding and blackmarketing.

It is a question of demand and supply that counts. If the demand increases and supply remains constant or falls, the price is bound to rise ushering in an era of inflation in its wake.

Comments: The candidate shows initiative, originality and courage to express his views freely and frankly. His arguments are rational and logical and he is sincere and earnest.

Interviewer: Do you think that nuclear power would be the right solution to India's mounting energy needs?

Piyush: Nuclear power has to be cost effective as compared to thermal, hydel, diesel or even solar power generation. India has abundant coal, water and offshore oil reservoirs and excellent solar resources, which still remain untapped, whereas nuclear power will prove costlier. Apart from these considerations, there is the risk of accidents and resulting nuclear radiation from nuclear power plants. They could also be the primary targets for enemy attacks during war with the attendant radiation and other risks. Hence, nuclear power generation has to be selective and woven into our total power plan.

Comments: The candidate reveals the ability to face a complex situation with imagination, analyze the major factors involved in their correct perspective, and decide the course of action to be followed in a firm and unambiguous manner to achieve successful results. His answer indicates that he is keeping himself abreast of current and latest developments in each field.

Interviewer: How do you react personally to the government decision to raise the retirement age of government servants and also to raise the upper age limit for recruitment to various services and posts?

Piyush: The government decision is based on the recommendations of the fifth pay commission. As the longevity has increased and old persons (more than 60 years old) now form about eight percent of our population, the retirement age is bound to be increased. Even then, the step is not an unmixed blessing. It means that for the next two years, there will be stagnation as there will be no retirement and no fresh recruitment. That will add to the frustration of the unemployed youth. Further, raising the recruitment age of civil services to 30 years for general candidates and 35 years for the reserved categories is on the high side. During the ICS days, the entry age was 21 years.

Comments: During his 35-minute long interview the candidate has fully convinced the Interviewer and the board members that he is a well-read and fully accomplished young man who has a clear-cut understanding of the various issues facing the country and is, therefore, a fit person to be in the administration as an administrative officer.

Interviewer: Well, Mr Piyush, now the interview can be deemed to have ended unless, of course, you have any queries on your side.

Piyush: Oh, thank you very much, Sir. I have no questions please. (He wishes the board good day and makes a smart exit)

NOTE: Opportunity to ask questions at this stage is useful, provided of course, the services are such as are well-known and no questions in such a case may be asked, as the interviewers would not be able to answer questions like targets for the next few years, place of posting, etc. and such a question is bound to put the interviewers in perplexity. It is with this view that we have avoided to make the candidate ask any questions.

Final Outcome: Mr Piyush is an enthusiastic, considerate and lively candidate who displays versatile interests and knowledge in many fields. He is very quick on the uptake and his grasp of various socio-economic factors is very swift and sharp. He has an analytical mind and an inquiring attitude. He has read extensively and taken special pains to keep himself well-abreast of all important national and international issues. He is self-confident, action-oriented, decisive and resolute. Selected with top honours.

8

A FINAL WORD

A Final Word

An interview is similar in many ways to a social conversation, but it requires more than just conversational skills. How well you do in an interview will depend on how well you can elaborate on your accomplishments and qualifications as they relate to what the organisation wants and needs.

Facing an interview is more of a talent than knowledge, which can be acquired. While your knowledge, academics and other qualifications play a major part in your assessment, the selection is still very much based on the judgment of the interviewer.

Interviewer decides whether to appoint you; not only on the basis of your credentials, but also on whether your persona will be healthy in their organisation. Often the interviewer's go with their gut feelings on who will get the job offer. Try to say what the interviewer wants to hear. Go ahead and analyze the situation yourself before you sit in front of him.

During an interview, a highly nasty discussion can be discussed about your previous job. Why are you leaving your present job? How do you evaluate your present organisation?

What do you think is an ideal working environment? Don't look panicked when questioned on them. A fine way to deal with the most obvious question on why you are quitting your current job can be made comfortable, if twisted to a group reason. Say a reason like our department was consolidated or eliminated. This will save you from direct exposure to the issue. Be sure you don't make stories. Act smart and prepare such answers in advance. Knowing the answer will make you comfortable in the uncomfortable situation also!

Have a positive attitude towards your present job. Don't look annoyed while describing your previous organisation. It can be a style of judgement that the recruiter is using to check your attitude. In reality, you could be absolutely heartbroken but hold your emotions. Be practical, the man you are talking to is not your girl friend that you can cry over all that went wrong. Take it all in the positive way.

To describe the best working condition according to you is just to know if you are meant for the organisation. Don't say people should be helpful, understanding and reliable. Talk from the organisation's point of view. Say you would be happy to work in a place where people are treated as fairly as possible. This is telling the recruiter how open you are to deal with tough situations. Interviewers need to be won over. They need to be convinced that you will be able to fix their troubles and help their company achieve its goals. One of the finest ways to answer interview questions is to use your career success stories. Career success stories are an account of the crucial instant in your career when you conquered important challenges to succeed. These stories will create unforgettable impression of you.

In particular, if you are being interviewed for a new field or new job, make connection between your exceptional abilities and associated situations in the new field through the success you have achieved in the past.

A Final Word

Interview—A Table Tennis Game

The effective way of behaving in an interview is to answer the questions you are asked in a concise manner without manipulation and without trying to avoid the questions asked. Similar to a table tennis game, the objective of each of the players is to pass the ball to the opponent's court. When an interviewer asks a question – answer precisely to what is being asked; return the ball to the interviewer's court. It seems that it is the simplest technique. However, a lot of interviewees are concerned that they may answer incorrectly and tend to respond either in a concise or in an irrelevant manner altogether.

Example A:

Interviewer: "What were you doing between 2006-2007?"
Applicant: "The truth is there is nothing important to say about these years. Yet, in 2007-2008 I was involved in projects that were much bigger and prestigious that may be of interest to you."

In this case the job applicant does not answer the question he or she were asked and creates a bad impression. The interviewer may think that the applicant is trying to avoid or hide an issue. The more your responses are concise and focused (not necessarily too short or brief) the better the impression you make. This may require some effort on your part, but it is definitely worthwhile.

Example B:

Interviewer: "Please describe your last position."
Applicant: "In my last position I managed a team of 8 computer programmers. I was managing a R&D project that developed a new instrument that discovers faults in airplane engines."

In this case, the applicant responds in a concise manner and answers the question he or she was asked.

Preparation

The single most important thing you can do to beat interview nerves is to be prepared. Worrying that you don't know enough is often the single biggest cause of nerves in interviewees. Research everything, not only about the company you are applying for, but also about the person who will be interviewing you (if this information is known). Having some sort of prior knowledge of your interviewer will not only make them seem more human and less like the terrifying monster you imagine in your head, but it will also inevitably show through in the interview and this will prove to be impressive.

Prepare confident answers to the obvious questions you will be asked and always twist your answers to show how you, above all other applicants, are ideally suited to the specific job in question. It may be helpful to practice an interview with someone you know, who will give you an honest and constructive feedback.

It is also important to prepare questions that you want to ask the interviewer, in order for them to sell the potential of their company to you. Not only will this reinforce the positive mindset achieved prior to the interview, but it explicitly shows the interviewer that you are keen to get this particular job and are confident enough to ask direct, assertive questions.

Change Your Mindset

The first step to beating this anxiety is to completely change your mindset concerning the interview. For most people, the interview is considered to be synonymous with an intense period of questioning, which allows the company to make judgements as to your suitability for the job. However, whilst this may be partially true, the interview is

A Final Word

also an opportunity for you to make similar judgements of the company. It is your only chance to find out whether working for this company will suit you. Once you adopt this mindset, you will regain the feeling of control, which is often lost as soon as people enter the interview room.

Forget Fear Of Interview For A Job

Change your thinking. The first and most important step is to change the way that you view the interview. You won't get the job, which may not have been the right job for you anyway.

Secondly, this is a conversation – a two-way process. You will be interviewing them as much as they are interviewing you. When you are not checking them out and learning what they have to offer, you are missing an opportunity that you may regret later.

Forget Fear Of Rejection

You may have had a number of interviews with no offer. You may be feeling defeated, and it's beginning to affect your self-esteem. This would be true of anyone. But it is a mistake to take it personally.

Let it go. Give yourself credit for getting an interview – only a small percentage of people get this far in the process. Give yourself credit for going out there and putting yourself in line, even though it is painful for you. Give yourself permission to not get job offers. Believe that an offer will come through when it is the right offer – the right fit for the company and for you. Take the control back and reject the feeling of fear.

When you have done everything to prepare for the interview, and you are satisfied that you can present yourself in the best light possible, the next step is for you to let it go. You can learn something from each interview. Learn to enjoy meeting new people and having new experiences. Who knows you may even grow to like interviewing.

Calming Techniques

One of the best techniques to handle stress is through breathing. Take deliberate, shallow breaths. Take air in through the nostrils and exhale quietly through your mouth. This is a technique that should be practiced as a relaxation technique before the interview so that your body gets used to slowing down the breathing process and relaxing.

Relaxation techniques such as yoga and meditation classes are recommended for anyone who has an extreme case of interview fright. The interview can cause panic attacks if the fear is strong enough. Pre-conditioning will do wonders for this type of anxiety.

Preparation Before The Interview

These are competitive times and you should steel yourself to expect some rejection. Well, you probably aren't going to get a job offer after every interview. For every job you apply for, there are more likely to be three to four equally qualified candidates in line for the same job. Whether you stand out from the crowd will depend on your preparation and ability to show confidence in yourself, believing that you are the 'best candidate for this job'. How can you possibly sell anyone anything if you don't believe in in yourself?

Preparation will make you feel more confident and less anxious.

A Final Word

1. Before the Interviews

- Conduct basic interview research
- Every interview must be preceded by research to give you an edge over the rest. Find out as much as you can about the company before the interview.

Here is a list of the information that you must have:

- Name of the interviewer
- Organisational structure
- Divisions/departments that interest you
- Products/services
- Training programs
- Size of the company
- Career paths
- How long have they been in business?
- Types of clients
- Growth in the past and future potential
- Job description and job title
- New products and services they are developing
- Employee benefits
- Geographic location of home office, branches, stores, etc.

2. Sample questions

Here is a list of common questions usually asked in an interview. Prepare them well.

- How would you describe yourself?
- What are your long-term and short-term goals and objectives and how are you preparing yourself to achieve them?

- What specific goals, other than those related to your occupation, have you established for yourself for the next 10 years?
- What do you see yourself doing five years from now?
- What are the most important rewards you expect in your career?
- What do you expect to be earning in five years?
- What do you consider to be your greatest strengths and weaknesses?
- Why should we hire you?
- Why did you choose this profession? What qualifications do you have that make you think that you will be successful in this field?
- How do you determine or evaluate success?
- What do you know about our organisation?
- Why did you decide to seek a position with this organisation?
- In what ways do you think you can make a contribution to our organisation?
- What qualities should a successful manager possess?
- Describe the relationship that should exist between a supervisor and those reporting to him or her
- What has been your biggest achievement and why?
- Tell us about your previous job experience. Reasons for leaving the previous job.
- Do you have a geographical preference?
- Will you relocate? Does relocation bother you?
- Are you willing to travel?
- Are you willing to spend at least six months as a trainee?
- Why do you think you might like to live in the community in which our organisation is located?

- What have you done that shows initiative?
- What major problems have you encountered, how did you deal with it and lessons that you have learnt out of them?

3. Organisation's expectations

Every organisation has a set of expectations from the prospective employee. In order to know that you fulfil those expectations, you must ask yourself the following questions:

- Do you have the skills to do the job?
- Do you fit in the organisation structure?
- Do you understand the company and its purpose?
- How do you stack up against the competition?
- Do you have the right mindset for the job and company?
- Do you have the right mindset for the job and company?
- Do you want the job?

4. Pick Your Outfit and Go to Bed Early

Lay out your interview outfit the night before and get a good night's rest, and start early. The last thing you want is to arrive at the interview flustered and panicked because you couldn't find the interview spot.

Be clear about the exact time, date and place of the interview and the contact name and position. Ensure you arrive 5 to 10 minutes early just to be safe.

The Day Of The Interview

Make sure that you have fully prepared your schedule for the day of the interview. Plan your route to the location of your interview a few days before and make sure you have a well thought out back up route in case of delays on your first route. In the morning, leave early to arrive at your destination. Having to hurry will only leave you feeling flustered and anxious. Decide what to wear the night before and then get an early night's sleep! It may be a good idea to take a sleeping remedy to ensure you get a full night's sleep. Your job interview outfit should be something you feel comfortable and confident in, but also makes you feel smart and successful enough to get any job. Eat a decent breakfast even if food is the last thing your stomach feels like having! Food will ultimately settle your nerves.

During the interview itself, one of the most important yet subtle things you can do to boost your self-confidence and banish any nerves, which may be, creeping up in you, is to have a confident smile. Smiling has scientifically proven benefits: it releases endorphins, which instantly make us feel better, and can even fake the brain into making you feel happier. It also gives the outward appearance of confidence and professional ease to the interviewer, even if you don't feel that comfortable inside! Ultimately, knowing that you appear more confident from the outside, you will feel less nervy from the inside.

At The Interview

> *Non-verbal messages * Focus on the handshake * Posture * Don't fidget * Maintain eye contact * Be comfortable * Listen attentively * Speak clearly * Be positive and enthusiastic*

Non-verbal Messages: Non-verbal language speaks larger than words. As you walk into the Interview Room, here are a few things that you must keep in mind. Start off like a winner.

The handshake: Offer your hand, and give a firm handshake, a pleasant smile and a positive and confident attitude. Introduce yourself.

Posture: Stand and sit erect.

Don't Fidget: There is nothing worse than people playing with their hair, clicking pen tops, tapping the feet, or unconsciously touching yourself.

Eye Contact: Look the interviewer in the eye.

Move your hands: Gesturing or talking with your hands is very natural, but keep it in moderation.

Be comfortable: Take a seat facing the interviewer, however, slightly away from the centre. Be sure that you are in a comfortable position.

Listen attentively: Look at the interviewer directly, but don't get into a stare down! Sit up straight. Try to relax. It's okay to take a few notes if the questions are lengthy or if you need to remind yourself of something you want to stress on.

Avoid nervous mannerisms. Pay attention to nervous mannerisms. Everyone is nervous to some extent; the key is to appear calm and composed.

Speak clearly: Use good grammar and a friendly tone. Never answer just "Yes" or "No" to a question. Always clarify, expand on your answers. Be sure not to go on rambling

Be positive and enthusiastic: Pump up your enthusiasm prior to the interview. Never whine, gripe or complain about past employers, jobs, classes, etc.

Ask pertinent questions. Be prepared to ask a few questions. Do not monopolise the interviewer's time, particularly if you know they have appointments scheduled following your interview. Do ask thoughtful questions. Don't ask about salary and benefits, this can be discussed when the company is definitely interested in you.

While Giving Answers To Questions

Be Concise: Listen to the questions carefully and answer to the point. An interviewee rambling on is likely to turn off the interviewer.

Provide Examples: Support your contentions with examples. Think of recent strong strategic examples of work you've done, then when the question is asked, answer with specifics, not in generalities.

Be Honest: It is always better to state the truth than beating about the bush. If you don't know something then state the fact.

Keep Your Guard: Always maintain your professionalism. Don't get swayed by the friendly behaviour of the interviewer and disclose everything. For all you know, it might be a trap laid out by him.

Winning Interview Technique

> * Dress appropriately * Be Punctual* Body language says a lot * Answer truthfully * Keep your cool

For a successful interview, you need to master a winning interview technique. It takes a lot of effort to write an impressive CV, to start with. This is your first step towards getting a call for an interview. Once your CV is screened for an interview, the interview technique has to be mastered. Planning is very important before attending an interview.

Facing an interview is not that difficult as it seems if you are well prepared for it. What is the master key to a great interview? Obviously, an unbeatable interview technique! The following guidelines will see you through the interview easily.

1. Dress appropriately

While attending an interview, a good way to impress is by dressing well for the occasion. Don't wear revealing outfits or jeans as they portray you as very casual and irresponsible. It is better to dress conservatively, unless the dress code is mentioned by the employers. One interview technique is to

A Final Word

try out a formal wear before the interview. Also, groom yourself with a good haircut and always present yourself in polished shoes.

2. Be Punctual

Punctuality is a virtue, which most employers look out for. Make sure that you reach the place of the interview, at least fifteen minutes before the scheduled time. This way you can acquaint yourself with the surroundings, and it will also show that you are committed with this interview technique. Keep in mind that you do not reach too early or too late.

3. Body language says a lot

The first time you meet the interviewer, give him a firm handshake. It gives a good impression about you. This is a sure-shot interview technique. Just like your verbal communication, you will be judged upon your non-verbal communication as well. Moreover, remember not to make excessive hand movements, slouch or play with your keys or a pen and stare at the interviewers' panel.

4. Answer truthfully

Your winning interview technique lies in being honest while answering the questions. Do not boast or emphasise your achievements and areas of expertise. The employers can figure out easily if you are lying about your career graph or anything else. Don't lie to them and just say no if you really cannot answer a question. That will show that you are sincere in your approach. Also, don't give an answer like you are reading a movie script. You should reply to the point and provide information that is required.

5. Keep your cool

It is natural to be a little tensed during an interview. Keep yourself relaxed and confident when answering the questions. In case you feel that the interviewer is not happy with your answers, do not get disturbed at all. A composed personality is supposed to have the right interview technique.

One more interview technique is that always ask your queries after the interview is over, when you have the chance to do so. The interviewers tend to pressurise candidates by asking different questions, just to check whether they can handle it. Follow the interview technique by being yourself and be successful.

The prospect of an imminent interview is enough to give anyone sleepless nights and cold sweats, and that's just before the interview. If this anxiety continues to the actual day of the interview, it can completely eliminate any chance of getting success at the interview. Fortunately, it is a very simple process to overcome these nerves and thus ensure you make the most of your interview.

Some Unusual Hints

One hint, which may work for you, is to imagine the interviewer in a different situation to that of the formal office. It can sometimes take a lot to realise that the interviewer is fundamentally the same as you – human. Therefore, it is perhaps useful to imagine them physically facing the same daily trials as you – sleeping through the alarm, arriving late at work because they couldn't find their keys, dropping some mayonnaise from the sandwich at lunch on their tie and so on.

Another hint, which you may not have thought of, is talking to yourself. Talk aloud before the interview while practicing your prepared answers and also do it during the interview (in your head of course)! Tell yourself mentally that you are the best applicant for this job and this is your chance to sell yourself. If you think you have answered a question well, mentally congratulate yourself. This may sound a bizarre technique but it can only give you confidence and help to mentally banish personally diminishing thoughts, which can result from shaky nerves.

9

AFTER THE INTERVIEW

After The Interview

Exit the interview as if you personally thought it was a complete success. Show a confident and assured smile and give a firm handshake. Some of this confidence is bound to transfer across to the interviewer and thus you will leave a positive last impression of yourself. Whether or not you feel that the interview was a success, try to put it completely out of your mind as soon as you have left the interview room. If you dwell too much on your performance it can negatively impact on subsequent job interviews you may have. Take confidence from the fact that even if you have failed this interview, it has still provided excellent practice for the next one. Prepare in exactly the same way for any upcoming interviews, but it is important to give yourself at least one night off to relax, instead of overloading your brain too much and thus multiplying nerves.

Some of the most important job interview techniques are:

- An excellent initial impression is an essential job interview technique as it exudes a favourable glow on everything else you say during the rest of the interview.

- An interview technique of interpreting body language is an important tool. For example, confidence is related to good posture and brisk gait.

- Good listening skills are an essential job interview technique – remain calm and collected and respond promptly when questioned.

- Proper preparation gives you an edge regarding job interview techniques but make sure that you interact well with the interviewer and don't succumb to memorised answers.

- An effective job interview technique is to adjust your speed of speech to match that of the interviewer and project a relaxed image.

- Do not make negative comments during the interview, a preferable job interview technique that greatly increases your chances of getting a job offer is projecting a positive, upbeat attitude and another effective job interview technique is adapting your answers to match the type of organisation you are being interviewed for.

- An important job interview technique is to follow the interview style established. For example, structured or unstructured and respond to the questions accordingly. Following the style will leave the interviewer with a more favourable impression about you.

- During the first meeting, emphasise one of your key, distinctive strengths as much as possible as a job interview technique. During later interviews, the job interview technique necessary is to present yourself as a well-balanced choice for the position.

- Keep up with the industry trends by reading trade publications and talk with industry insiders – a job interview technique that will lead to success.

- Have prior knowledge of the company – a job interview technique that gives you an added advantage.

- Invading your privacy can be illegal. An interview technique is to gracefully point out that the question is illegal and decline to respond or calmly refer to the question making you uncomfortable.
- Be prepared for an interview – keep your resume and alphabetised company dossiers in a nice folder, a good job interview technique and always remain calm, poised and positive.

Some Probable Questions And Answers

Q. 1. Tell us something about yourself. What can you tell us about yourself? It may come in many variations but is usually the icebreaker in an interview.

Quite often the first question that the interviewer asks is, "Tell me something about yourself." Most candidates feel that this is a silly and very simple question because all the details are already mentioned in the resume that is before the interviewer. Some also make the mistake of taking this question as very easy. In fact, it is not so.

Why is the question asked?

The interviewer has a number of reasons for asking this question. He wants the candidate to relax a little, be natural, because this is one subject about which every candidate's knowledge level is the same. However, the candidates must remain on guard against getting too relaxed also. Many candidates let down their defenses completely, after this question. Do not forget that every word you say here is leaving a bearing on the final outcome of the interview.

This question also helps the interviewer to test your communication skills, your self-confidence and above all your self-esteem. A candidate who talks more about his relatives and less about himself may be suffering from a sense of poor self-esteem. Your answer must, very briefly, touch upon your family background and then go on to the professional side of your training and education. You must highlight those attributes, hobbies and habits that are likely to help you do a good job. Following could be an answer to this first question.

A sample answer is suggested here. You must fit your true details in this framework. The point to be noted is that the focus must be on you and not on your family, teachers, etc. You may begin with what you are doing presently and may then go back to what you have accomplished before. Lay more emphasis on matters that have more relevance to the job that you are going to do and on facing the interview. If the interviewer does not stop you, you can use this opportunity to talk briefly about your strengths, hobbies and also why you chose this career.

Answer: I am ... (Tell your name), I am doing ... (Tell your present occupation). My early education took place in ... (Name the college) in ... (Name the city where this college is located) and then I completed my ... (Graduation and post graduation) from ... My parents and other family members have always drilled into me the virtues of honest hard work. I have always tried to maintain a balance between sports and studies during my student days. My academic record is ... and I did ... (Mention some of your achievements as a student).

I was a keen about cricket and even captained the college cricket team. I have always been a good team player and generally get along well with people. I always believe that one must protect one's rights without stepping on the rights of others also. We can work together only if we believe in and strive for a win-win situation.

Ever since I reached my graduation level, I have been thinking of working in (name the industry). I have keenly observed the growth of this industry. I have been trying to gain the skills required to do this job well. For example, you may have undertaken some short-term courses or attended

After The Interview

some lectures or read some relevant books. You must present these facts to the interviewer and you must mention how this might help you to do a better job. In case the company is a leading or well-known player in the field, you could add that you have been nourishing a dream of joining this company.

Remember not to give long examples or stories to the answer in this question but do briefly touch upon the things mentioned above. Do not forget to keep looking at the interviewer to see signs of boredom or irritation. You may give a short pause after completing a sentence, if the interviewer does not start talking it means he, perhaps, wants you to tell more. He may show this with a nod of his head, also. Be careful that you don't highlight unnecessary details. When the competition is stiff, even minor issues can make the difference between the selection and rejection. For example, once a candidate revealed inadvertently that he had spent a day in a hospital as he had been wrongly diagnosed as having hypertension. The interviewer never told him anything but this information played in his mind against the candidate. A doubt was sown in his mind that may be, just may be, he might be suffering from the disease. You have to be continuously alert on what is going to improve your chances of selection and what is going to hamper them.

Q. 2. What is your favourite subject?

Why is the question asked?

Clearly if you can't be good in the subject which is your favourite, how can you be expected to be good in the subject that you don't like much? Now this can be both a trap and also an opportunity.

Well, before the interview you must think about which subject you really can call your favourite. In this subject you would do well to revise the basics, which probably you might have forgotten. The interviewer would really like to know how well you have grasped the basics of the subject you call your favourite. He may not expect you to go in deep details nor may there be enough time for that, but he will expect you to know the basic concepts.

Be sure about one thing, it is a serious mistake to pretend to know what you don't know. If you don't know something accept it and at the same time if you know something connected to the topic, you could say that you know this but not that. If you are not sure you could try and add that you think it is this, or you may give the reply as such but if you don't know about the subject do not claim so.

Q. 3. What are your hobbies?

Why is the question asked?

Your hobbies tell a lot about your personality, your upbringing, your beliefs, etc. You must be in a position to mention a few of your hobbies clearly. However, you had to better gather more information about your hobbies.

It is somewhat like your favourite subject. It is an invitation to another question. Suppose you mention reading as your hobby, the next question may be what are you reading at present or what have you read in the past one week or so? Similarly, if you mention some sport as your hobby the interviewer is quite likely to ask you about some rules of the game or recent events in the game. Knowing the names of some of the players of that game might also be very desirable. This will also give an indication that even to your hobbies you are sincere.

Q. 4. What motivates you?

Why is the question asked?

This is another way of probing your attitude. The interviewer wants to know whether your sources of motivation come from inside or you need outside factors to motivate you. He may also like to know as to how well you understand your

After The Interview

motivating factors. How clear you are about what motivates you is a sure indication of how well-motivated you are.

Answer: You must mention the motivating factors, which are likely to be present in the assignment, which you are looking forward to undertake. For example, if it is a large and old established company then quick promotion may not be realistic and you should not aim for that. Instead, you may say that the respect with which people or customers look at your company and at you motivates you. This would go well with the reality of this company. Similarly, if it is a field job where you are likely to work without much direct supervision you could say that you are motivated by the trust, faith and freedom that is exhibited by the company and you would like to deliver the goods to show that you can take responsibility when it is given. Let us take the case of a job in an office set up where the boss is likely to reward or reprimand you for all the tasks assigned to you. You could say that you like to be patted when you have done a good job and certainly you would like to be corrected when you haven't delivered up to the standards.

Q. 5. Who is your hero?

Why is the question asked?

This is a hidden way of knowing the philosophy of your life and work. You certainly like a person who is similar to what you dream of becoming. The type of hero you have tells the interviewer in a subtle way what you want in life and what you worship or stand for.

Answer: What you have to do is highlight the positive a little more and underplay the negative, a little. Consciously scan your thoughts and think of what can be more relevant to the interviewer. With respect to having a hero, usually we never have given it a conscious thought. Usually, we mention the latest heartthrob of Bollywood or the sports arena as our hero, simply because he is the name you are able to recall at that moment. Now is the time to give it a serious conscious thought.

When you are talking to a professional corporate manager you must mention a hero who is connected to the industry, corporate world and has come up in a hard way. Come to think of it, no one will deny such a person being a hero but if you don't give it a conscious thought beforehand you might not be able to recall a name at the crucial time. Moreover, you will be expected to know a little more about a person whom you consider a hero. So, go through the lives of some of the most respected industrialists and corporate managers. Decide who should be your hero and why. Now that you have chosen your hero, do more research on him. Try to know more about his life. Try to remember some anecdotes, which prove that your liking is not just a fancy but based on certain values and principles.

Q. 6. What are your strengths?

Why is the question asked?

This is a vague question but asked cleverly with specific purpose. The basic idea is to know how honest you are to yourself besides being in a position to convert your weaknesses into your strengths. You could be more elaborate and talk more about your strengths. However, even here you must not lose focus of the job requirements and must lay more emphasis on those strengths, which are relevant to the job profile.

Very often, the interviewer may ask you to elaborate upon your strength. He may connect your reply to another question so you should be ready for that. For example, if you say you are very innovative, the interviewer could ask you how has your innovativeness benefited your previous organisation or what specific incident of your life has made you to believe that you are innovative. Suppose you say that you are a good student and pick up new concepts quickly, the interviewer may seek to know what percentage of marks have you been getting and he may also ask you to give an example that can prove that you pick up new concepts fast.

Always keep your examples ready while replying to this question. For example, suppose you say that one of your strengths is that you can adjust to new systems or situations easily. You may be asked to give an example when you demonstrated this quality to the benefit of your previous employer. You could dig up your memory and find an example when you did something in tune with that strength. If you claim that you have this strength certainly something must have happened that has formed this opinion in you. You could have helped your boss in something that was not really your job but which benefited the organisation.

Another variant of this question might be, "There are so many candidates, what is so special about you or why should we select you?"

Q.7. What are your weaknesses?

Why is the question asked?

Naturally this question follows the one on strengths. The reason is again, to know how you feel about yourself. How do you assess yourself in terms of your weaknesses as well as strengths?

The answers to this question run to various extremes usually. While one person may say that he is full of strengths and devoid of any weakness, another may say the opposite, that he has a few strengths but many weaknesses. It is almost funny to see people straining a lot while they recall their strengths but rattle their weaknesses in a stream. While both extremes are not appreciable the latter one is worse than the former.

Ideally, the answer should be well-balanced; you must strike a good balance while underplaying your weaknesses and slightly overplaying those strengths, which can help you, do a good job. Some of your weaknesses may at times help you do a better job; you could sell them packaged in that way.

Answer: In answer to the question on weaknesses, you may give a slight pause as if you were straining to think about it. Then mention one or two weaknesses and lay more emphasis on the one that may help you do a good job. For example, you could say that you do not tolerate mediocrity and tend to lose your temper when people do a careless job, though sometimes it may be good, it has spoiled your relations at times. Also, show that you are fully aware about the implications of your weakness and are working on it.

The main thing is that; do not rattle out your weaknesses too much. You must underplay them a little. A little humour may be of help here. You could start by giving out a very flimsy weakness like eating pickle (be careful, resort to humour only if you have established a good rapport with your interviewer already). Switch quickly to seriously answering the question rather than continuing with your joke.

Q. 8. Why do you want to leave your present employer?

Why is the question asked?

Push or pull. The interviewer wants to know whether your present employer is pushing you out or the company interviewing you is pulling you in. In other words, either you are not doing well enough in your present job and are hence, thinking of a change or this company is attracting you towards itself because of something very positive about it. They may also want to know whether you will leave this organisation also, for the same reason one day. Since the interviewer would like you to come over for a long-term employment, the clarification is necessary.

Let us see what can be your reason for seeking a change in job. It could be one or more of the following:

- You could be looking for a higher salary. You could be looking for a higher post.
- You may not like the place were you are working now.

- There could be something wrong with the boss, in your opinion.
- There could be some problem with your colleagues.
- You may fear the failure of the business.
- The company may be sacking you.
- The company may be winding up.
- The company may be changing your department.
- You might have been transferred to a distant location.
- You are not happy with some aspect of your working life in the organisation.

You would do well to convince the interviewer that you would not leave just because of a flimsy reason. The reason whatever it may be must be serious and not frivolous. Nobody wants an immature or unstable employee. You must demonstrate that you have thought of long-term prospects. Always show orientation towards long-term vision. Career decisions should never be based on short-term considerations and you must reflect this understanding and maturity in your replies.

Q. 9. What according to you is an ideal job?

Why is the question asked?

The interviewers want to know as to how well your ideas fit into the profile of the person they are looking for. He would also like to know whether you are applying for this job just because you are not getting a job anywhere else or is it that you really want to do this sort of work. This question also tests the clarity of your thought process, your priorities in life, etc.

You must try to be as realistic as possible. The ideal job described by you must be close to the job profile you have applied for. Yet, if there are some minor differences you may mention those also to make your answer more realistic, but do not highlight major differences. For example, if you are going for an accounting job and you say that in your ideal job you must deal with speaking to a lot of new people, travelling a lot for work, etc. This will mean that your basic profile does not seem to match the requirements of the job you have applied for. You could say that in your ideal job you should deal with numbers, running against deadlines and good career growth prospects. The last one may not be really available in a typical accounting job but is a minor deviation. If questioned on that you can always say that if you go for the right type of professional courses while on job you can rise fast in your career. This will be true, especially if you are talking to a large company. A small organisation may not take kindly to your giving exams while on their payroll and may also not like to take a very ambitious person. They may feel that you would not stick to the job very long.

The same question may be asked in another way i.e., "Given a choice which profession would you like to choose?"

Such questions pose the danger of catching you off guard in the sense that you may venture into deeper areas of your mind and reveal feelings, which are not in tune with the requirements of this job.

Q. 10. What are your long-term career goals? Or where do you see yourself five years or ten years from now?

Why is the question asked?

The interviewer would like to know how ambitious, positive and forward looking you are. He would also like to check as to whether your long-term goal can be satisfied within the organisation or would you need to change the organisation. There may be some rare organisations, typically charity organisations, trading houses, etc., which may not be looking for people for long-term employment but most of the organisations hire people with a long-term perspective in mind. Therefore, your reply should talk of an aim that can be filled within the organisation and the fulfilment of which may benefit the organisation also. For example, if you say that your aim is to earn enough money and go abroad, will it benefit the organisation? Or, if you say that you plan to work for two years, gain some experience and then branch out into a business of your own, they will certainly not like that. They will also not like you to leave the job and go for some higher studies or to keep trying for civil services or MBA while you are working for them. Your aim should appear realistic, achievable and must not be over-ambitious. It must not be out of sync with your qualifications, abilities or objectives of the organisation.

Your answer could revolve around doing a good job, learning everything about the business, being in good books of the management, getting at least two promotions in five years and earning enough money to be at par with the best among your peers.

Answer: For example, you could say, "Sir, I am looking forward to learning as much as possible about this job. I want to be the best in this field. Naturally I am ambitious, but I know that only when I do very well in my present job, will I be suitably rewarded monetarily as well as in terms of growth in my career. The way I look at things today is that I expect to go at least two steps higher in the hierarchy in a period of 5 years from now. Financially, I would want to be at par with the best in my category. I am convinced that if I learn my job well, apply my mind and all my talent to do a good job, all the rewards will automatically come to me".

Q. 11. What is required to be successful?

Why is the question asked?

Now this question must take you back to professional success and is not about the more philosophical aspect of success. The interviewer wants to see your clarity of thought and how focused you can be towards success. Of course, the same principles that make you successful in your job will also help you to succeed in other fields.

Answer: Your answer must show your clarity of thought, a deep sense of purpose, self-discipline, confidence in yourself, and ability to express your ideas clearly.

You may say, "I feel that a clear objective, a strong will to achieve that goal, proper skills, ability to learn from mistakes of self as well others, a time-bound program, a single-minded approach will all contribute to one's success."

You may have gone through the mock interviews already and may find this a repetition. However, this is specifically to clarify and fine-tune your own ideas and thoughts. When you think loudly as to why this is the right job for you, you discover new reasons and arguments to state that you are the right candidate

Q. I2. What is your life's philosophy?

Why is the question asked?

This is a variation of the earlier question, but goes beyond the professional sphere. Usually, if the interviewer has asked the earlier question he may not ask this one and vice-versa.

Answer: You will show a balanced approach towards life. You will focus more on professional success but will also emphasise that the basic reason for life is much higher and while being focused on one's career one must also keep the broad picture of the world in mind. It is true that only when you are a successful person you can be of any help to society and the environment.

Your reply could be, "I believe that personal success in one's chosen field is most crucial. However, one needs to maintain a good balance between one's job, home, health and society. We can call our life a balanced success only if we succeed on all these parameters."

You can also add that you believe that success comes when we work with dedication towards an extremely cherished goal. But happiness comes only when we are satisfied with what we get from life. We must have dreams and aspirations but we must also be thankful when something goes well for us. So, happiness is basically an attitude and that happiness has to come from the inside only.

Q. 13. What is your work philosophy?

Why is this question asked?

It is again a variation of the question on ambition. But it could be broader and less specific. It is more about the values that have been fed into you by your parents, teachers or other environmental factors. You are being tested for your attitude towards life and work. The interviewer wants to know your response to various challenges thrown by life at you.

Answer: You must emphasise again that you believe in giving and contributing the best possible as per your capabilities. You are convinced that if the person does well enough in his present work and learns more about the job of his boss, he will automatically get rewarded, financially as well as career wise.

You must sincerely believe and make known this belief that hard work has no substitute and success achieved by flukes does not stay for long. One day your real talent is challenged and if you have not come up in life while learning and falling on the way you will not be able to give a good fight.

I believe strongly in working hard and living well. You would certainly want your family to enjoy a good standard of living and you don't mind working hard.

You must also show your orientation towards achievement of results rather than just focusing on the activities. Perfection is fine but only as much as is required for the organisation to do well.

Q. 14. How do you handle challenges? Slight variation of the above question:

What is the most challenging situation you have ever faced?

Why is the question asked?

If you have reached this far in the interview, it is a very good sign. The interviewer is probably trying to get more material to be able to make up his mind. It is no doubt a chance for you to sell yourself better. For example, when you may ask a salesman in a showroom about how a product may work under extreme conditions, it means that you have accepted that the product seems good under normal circumstances. If there is a panel of interviewers it could also mean that the questioner is beginning to like you and is giving you a chance to prove yourself to other panel members.

Answer: An example will come in extremely handy at this stage also. It may be something that you did at home, at college or in your job; certainly everyone has had his share of challenges in life. Please recall a few incidents and record them.

Your answer must convey in some way that you remain cool under crisis situations, look at various options available, keep an open mind for innovative and unconventional solutions, evaluate the pros and cons of various options and then decide as to how you must go about it. Add to that an example when you handled a crisis well and you got through.

Q. 15. What do you know about us?

Why is the question asked?

The interviewer wants to know how much research you have done for the job, which in turn tells him about how serious you are about this job. It also is a pointer to your habit of going into details of a thing and taking your task seriously.

You must have researched enough about the company to be able to answer this question confidently. Not only should you give the information you should also mention the source of the information.

You could say, "I have read in the last month's Business Today that the market share of the company is 30% in the market with so many competitors. Also, your website talks about the new products you have recently launched and the growth prospects for future. In your company's last year's annual report, I have noticed that you have invested heavily in R&D and have also entered into collaborations with some foreign companies. All this tells me that the growth opportunities and challenges that your company is likely to throw up in the next ten years or so are great and unmatched."

You could also add (if you have taken the pains to do so) that you have met some employees of the company or some dealers and they have given you a lot of positive feedback about the company. You could also talk about the customer satisfaction levels with the company's quality or service.

This question might also come to you with some variation and depending upon the interviewer it may be put in different words. For example, he could ask you, "What do you know about this job? What do you know about this industry?"

The above two questions are also very common but are connected with the earlier question on your knowledge about the company. To answer such questions you need to do thorough study about the company.

Q. 16. Why do you want to join us?

Why is the question asked?

The interviewer through this question wants to know how clear you are about your objectives, how long you are likely to work in the place, what is your long-term and short-term plans. The interviewer may also be interested in knowing whether you have done some research about the company and how serious you are about the job.

Naturally, your answer should address the need of the interviewer, which in this case is that he wants a committed employee who is joining the company enthusiastically and with his eyes wide open. You have to convince the interviewer that you intend to stay for a long time.

Answer: You could say something like, "Your company is one of the fastest growing companies in this segment and I know that if I do well I can build my long-term career with your company. In the December issue of (relevant trade magazine name) I have read (some facts) about your company. From your website I have come to know that you train your employees very well and believe mostly in internal promotions. The speech of your President, which I read in the annual report of last year, has talked about making the field of telecommunication the major thrust area for your company. If I understand correctly this means that the company's growth is going to continue in that order. I feel that for my career I must work with a company that is growing fast and commands the respect of its customers."

This is one example of how you can demonstrate how much research you have undertaken to find out more about the company. You are also stating that you are not making the statement just to please the interviewer but is actually talking based on data and facts.

Your reply should state clearly that you have done your homework well and have decided that this is the best company to work for and that is why you have come for the interview. If you have any doubts about the company's future, please keep them to yourself during the interview. You must not show that you are in a double minds about working for the company. If you want to know more, you can always ask someone else or find out from some other source but please do not share the doubts with your interviewer.

Remember that your answer to this question must not show any doubt in your mind about your willingness to join the company. You must show a keen desire, but must not appear very desperate about getting the job. There is a fine line between desiring something and being desperate for it. Any deal can take place only if both parties feel benefited. Similarly, your interviewer should also feel that you as well as the company both are going to be benefiting from the deal. Your job is to convince the interviewer that you are the right candidate for the job. You make it obvious that the company needs you as much as you need the company.

Q. 17. Why should we hire you?

Why is the question asked?

This question can mean many things and is usually a good signal. This is an opportunity given to you by the interviewer to sell your candidature. This may also help you to identify your strengths but you would do well to talk about those strengths that are more relevant to the job profile. So, does it mean the same as the question what are your strengths? In a way yes but no, it does not mean the same thing. This is a more specific question where you are supposed to specify how your strengths are going to help you do a better job than others do. Please note the words, than others, which mean that you may not talk of non-specific attributes, which all or most of the others do.

For example, if you are going for an interview for a sales job, the fact that you are a creative person with artistic approach may not carry much weight. But could you mention that since you have participated in many art exhibitions or stage plays, you are a very popular person in the city where you are going to work. Also, this exposure to the public has made you very comfortable in facing new people. So the answer to this question should not only detail your qualities but also talk about how those qualities are going to help you do a better job, if selected.

Answer: You could say something like this, "I feel you should select me because of two reasons; one because I am locally very popular since I have participated in many stage shows during my college days, secondly I have worked in a similar position before as a part-timer, therefore I know how important it is to bring a continuous revenue to a business of this kind." You should be as specific as possible, in mentioning that you are going to bring more profits, revenue or customers to the company. Remember the company is hiring every employee, even the gatekeeper for profits only. So we must show our orientation towards profits, sale, customer satisfaction, etc.

Q. 18. How can we be sure that you will work with us for a long time?

Why is the question asked?

This question may be asked in various variations by interviewers. For example, where do you see yourself in five years from now, what is your long-term aim or what is your ideal job may be some variations of the same question. At least the purpose behind asking such questions is the same.

Your interviewer wants to know as to whether you are clear that you want to stay with this job or company for a long time or are not very sure. Naturally, the candidate who appears confused on the issue will stand less chance of getting selected than the person who shows no doubts at all. In any case, even if you have some doubts they should not be expressed at this stage. You can always clarify those doubts later.

Answer: "You see, at present what I am looking forward to is a good learning atmosphere and a platform to prove my talents. I am sure that in this job I will be able to fulfil my aspirations. I am full of enthusiasm and new ideas about how to do this job well. Therefore, I am sure that there will not be any need for change unless something goes drastically wrong. As such, I would definitely like to contribute as much as I can to the organisation that gives me a chance at this stage of my career."

You must not appear desperate for the job but you must express a burning desire to work for the Company or the position you have applied for.

Q. 19. What would you say if I abuse you? Another slight variation of the same question could be, What if a customer hits you or abuses you?

Why is the question asked?

This is a question testing your sense of self-esteem and self-respect. I suggest that you should not compromise on that. You must clearly show them that you have drawn a line between commitment to personal life and professional life.

Answer: If a customer or manager behaves in a manner that is not professional and hurts your personal dignity, you should treat him just the way you would treat any person doing that. It ceases to matter that the person in question is your boss or customer. However, you must remember that he is a human being and we should behave with dignity in spite of a provocation. Just because he is behaving in an uncivilised manner doesn't mean that we also have to do the same. You must say that you would remind the person that this sort of behaviour is unacceptable, uncivil and unprofessional. You can ask the person to limit his comments to professional matters and not to insult you personally. If the person still does not stop, you have to warn him that you would be forced to go to a higher authority if the uncivil act continues and you certainly must assertively carry out that threat. What you must not do nor say that you will do is to reply in the same coin because one crime clearly does not justify another.

Q. 20. If we offer you the position of ... ?

Why is the question asked?

It could be a trap. Be careful!

You may have shown very clear goals. And you may have spoken clearly about why you wanted this job. Now your interviewer is offering you something, which is almost equally good or better, but it is difficult for you to go back. Remember most of the time it is a trap. For example, if you have said that you want to work in the production department because you feel that you can use your technical expertise there. Now your interviewer is offering you a position in marketing at a higher salary in the city office, which is much better than the village where the production facilities are located.

Now, it is almost certain that the interviewer will not change his mind in the course of the interview and this is just a hypothetical question to judge your real sense of commitment.

Another possible hypothetical question is often on location. You may have said in the interview that you are willing to work anywhere. Now the interviewer suddenly informs you that they would like to send you to the northeast, where you certainly don't want to go.

You have to decide whether you would like to take the risk or not, but basically these questions should be treated like a hoax.

Q. 21. What will you do if we don't select you? Or it may be worded as, how do you handle failure?

Why is the question asked?

It is simply asked to find out as to how you handle stress and failure. How do you define courage? Courage is defined as grace at the time of adversity. So the interviewer would like to see whether you would be able to preserve your grace under the circumstances.

Many candidates, when told that they have not been selected, use statements like, "Oh! I knew it already; I just came because my mom insisted. I knew I wasn't good enough." Or worse still, "This was just an eye wash, I am told you had already selected the person or I just don't have any influential references."

If the interviewer says at the end, "We will inform you." Many candidates shoot back verbally or otherwise "I know what that means."

Do not use any such statements at all. They not only damage the ego of the interviewer they will also damage your own self-respect because deep down you know that all this may not be true.

Your answer must indicate that you will try to learn from this failure and will do better in future. Your resolve to get this job will be strengthened because it is challenging your qualities and competence. You need to improve and do better in future.

Answer: "I am quite confident that I shall be selected but in case I am not, I am prepared for that also. I will feel bad no doubt about that, but that won't be the end of the road. I will try to learn where I might have gone wrong. I will discuss with my seniors, my parents and I will definitely improve."

Q. 22. What is your town preference, if you are given a choice?

Why is the question asked?

Mobility is an important requirement of the corporate world. Even in positions where you may never be likely to move out of your home town the interviewer would prefer to take a person who is mobile. The reasons are two – one, mobility is an attitude more than anything else, and two you never know the circumstances might force the company to change location or staff placements. Therefore, an interviewer would always like to give some advantage to mobility. Of course, mobility is a must in sales jobs, field jobs and in companies with many locations.

In case you are absolutely sure that the position is in the town of your choice, then consider the possibility that the interviewer may be just testing you on this factor. If that were expected then perhaps it would be better to express full mobility. Mobility does mean that the person is willing to accept change, willing to adjust to new environment, etc.

Answer: I feel that you should be clear about how mobile you can really be and be frank enough about it. It is no point getting the job and not joining just because of the location. It would be advisable to be mobile and give full expression to your mobility. However, you may have to take into account practical considerations and you must decide your own priorities. Lack of mobility is perceived generally as a sign of unwillingness to take risks and go through new things in life, etc.

In case the reasons for your not being mobile are genuine and understandable it might be a good idea to explain them. They should not however indicate a weak mind or a person unwilling to take a risk. They should also not be the usual clinches like "My sister is getting married." More serious reasons, which the interviewer can also appreciate, may be mentioned. In case your difficulty is temporary and is likely to be over after a short time you can explain that also.

Q. 23. What will you do if your subordinate reaches late?

Why is the question asked?

This is a question for supervisory positions, normally but may be asked of the other candidates also at times. The problem of late arrival is just one example of any other issue of indiscipline or insubordination. The interviewer is trying to judge your skill level for this job.

The interviewer will also like to know whether you can tackle the problems on your own or would you seek the help of your boss or senior in tackling the problem. One more thing that you have to remember while answering such a question is that you should be guided by your principles,

After The Interview 163

values and the company policy rather than by opportunism and shortcut manipulative solutions.

Answer: For any such problem of indiscipline, you have to make it clear that you will not accept it. You must also make it clear that you are not going to run for cover to your boss for such routine issues. You may say that you will take his suggestion or feedback if the problem persists but the solution will have to be found and implemented by you only.

While tackling the problem you will say that you will tackle the human angle separately from the professional angle. You will give the person enough opportunity to improve.

You will increase the reprimand gradually if the problem persists and the person does not show improvement. You will start with a counseling session wherein you will try to understand the problems and explain to the employee that this behaviour would not be tolerated. You will also explain in clear terms to the employee what will be the result if the person does not change his habit of coming late or whatever other deviation may be there.

Q. 24. How have you contributed to the company that you worked for?

Why is the question asked?

This is an opportunity if you are prepared for it. If you are not prepared for this question it could prove to be your undoing. Because definitely you must have contributed in many ways to the employer with whom you are now working or with whom you have worked earlier. However, these contributions may be a routine or achieved over a period of time so you may take time to put them in perspective. That is why you should prepare yourself well for this question. You must dig deep into your memory and think of the overall measurable improvements that you may have brought about during your tenure at the company. The key is measurable results with an impact on revenue generation or customer satisfaction in the long-term or short-term. For example, you may have started the culture of sending a thank you note to every customer as soon as the dealer has confirmed a sale to you. Similarly, you may have started a trend of reacting quicker to a complaint and thus reducing the customer's waiting time. You may have done some special exercises, which might have fetched new customers to the organisation you worked for.

Remember that you must show a market, customer and profit orientation in every answer as far as possible. Times are very competitive and every employer's mind is pre-occupied with turnover, profits and customer satisfaction. You must show that you are also similarly pre-occupied.

If you have done some good or creative work in your earlier employment you could carry it along and even leave it there, if possible.

Q. 25. What if your boss gives you a deadline that is impossible to meet?

Why is the question asked?

It is asked to judge your assertiveness. Your ability to put forward your viewpoint even when you know that it may not be a very popular one. Your interviewer may also want to check how you handle pressure.

Answer: You can also not say that I will accept the impossible deadline. You can not also say that you will refuse to do the work. What you will do instead is that you will take the work but inform your boss very coolly that in your opinion the job can not be completed within the stipulated time. You may also add that if you were given an assistance or support, whatever may be required, and then you would be able to complete the work. You should sincerely believe that if you give it your best then it might be possible to complete it. Usually, the work is not as difficult as it appears at first sight. You can also add that if the boss, who is likely to be more experienced, has given the task it could be due to two reasons. One, due to the urgency of the work he feels that by giving such a deadline he expects the maximum possible output in the shortest time and two, by giving such a deadline he is raising the benchmark in the workplace. In any case, the only option one must consider is to do one's best and just give the boss your opinion about the nature of the difficulty.

Q. 26. What can we look forward to from you?

Why is the question asked?
Such a question will normally be asked of experienced persons who are likely to have a significant impact on the bottom-line of the company.

This may be like a case study; you would do well to seek more information before going in to the specifics of the job.

Answer: You could start the answer by saying that as far as activities are concerned you would do more than expected and would set new standards. However, as far as specific achievements are concerned you would need more information to be able to say in concrete terms what improvements you could achieve.

Q. 27. Where else have you been interviewed? Or which other company has interviewed you?

Why is the question asked?
The interviewer may like to know whether you have really been focused in your job search or have been appearing for all kinds of jobs. For example, you may have during this interview expressed clearly a desire to work for a bank or financial services organisation, but while mentioning the names of companies where you have gone for the interview, you may mention names of pharmaceutical or FMCG companies. This will show the interviewer that you are

desperately looking for whatever jobs you may get and are not clear about your aim.

The interviewer will also hope that while answering this question you might touch upon why you have been rejected by earlier interviewers which might give him a clue about you which he had not got till now.

Answer: Your answer must certainly not show you as an idle person doing nothing. You must come across as a person, who knows what he wants, who is carefully picking the sector and organisation he wants to work in. Don't give a long list of companies where you have been interviewed. Instead, name a few selected ones. Do not talk ill of or belittle the other companies or their management, etc for not recognising your talent. It will be better if you say that you have tried to learn from each experience and hope to pick up whatever skills are required by these companies.

Q. 28. Can you work in a team? Or, have you worked in a team before?

Why is the question asked?

Usually, such questions are asked during the wrap up of a more successful interview. With these questions the interviewer may like to confirm that he has selected the right person. It is possible that the interviewer is unable to reach a decision and he is just looking for some more convincing reasons to select you.

Answer: Remember that teamwork is definitely a prerequisite for accomplishing any task in the corporate world. There are hardly any projects or tasks that you can do all by yourself without any help from anyone. If you have experience of working in a team, mention it. If you don't have corporate work experience you can quote some examples from college life or even from family life. Family life is also a great experience in successful teamwork.

For successful working of a team, each member should have respect for the other; if there is a conflict it should be regarding the task and not a person. There should be a well-defined goal or mission. Responsibilities and roles should be clearly understood and agreed upon by each member of the team. The various members of the team should communicate with each other frequently and truthfully. In case of differences of opinion one person should have the authority to decide.

Q. 29. Can you adjust to our work culture? The question might be differently worded to include 'our location' or 'our methods', etc.

Why is the question asked?

Whether you are working or have just completed your studies you have been living a particular type of life under a particular set of conditions. The interviewer has a concern that when those circumstances change, how will you react? To be selected, you will have to address this concern of the interviewer. For example, if you have just completed your studies and have never in your life lived away from your parents you would be used to the great housekeeping of your mother. Now, suppose the new job will require you to work 10 hours a day in the heat, five hundred kilometers away from your home with all the household work also to be handled by you.

Answer: Naturally, the interviewer needs to be convinced that you will be able to accept the change and will not give up because of these minor problems. If you have good support from your parents or other relatives you must mention it, this can matter a lot. For example, if you are being sent away from home but your mother is likely to accompany you or if you have relatives in the town where you are being sent, this fact must be mentioned by you. Similarly, you may have gone for summer camps, NCC camps or hiking trips, etc., during your college days. You must mention these facts because they may help you to convince the interviewer that you are indeed going to manage living away from your parents.

Q. 30. What salary do you expect?

Why is the question asked?

In case you are working somewhere and you are clear about your priorities and the salary you want then, the answer should be straight forward, "At present, I am getting this much, and I am in good books of the management. I am likely to get a promotion next year with a handsome increment. I feel that I should be paid a minimum salary of this much. Though your company has a much better reputation and I wish to work with you, yet I feel that at least a hike of 20% (or whatever you may have asked for) is reasonable."

In case you are a fresher, you should communicate clearly that you would like to learn the job well. You could say that at this stage of my career what I learn is much more important than what I earn. You must make it clear that you believe in giving more to the organisation. You are confident that when you contribute to the growth and success of the organisation, the organisation will naturally take good care of you.

You could also add that you are not looking at your earnings today. You want to rise fast, learn new things and after doing a good job you are looking for a good salary three years down the line.

Q. 31. How will your boss react when you resign?

Why is the question asked?

This is to test your realism, how realistically you see situations and how well you understand them.

Howsoever tempted you may be to claim that your boss will commit suicide, please do not claim that. You must mention the inter-personal nature of your relationship with your boss.

Answer: No doubt the work I am doing is important. My boss as well as my colleagues in the department will certainly

After The Interview 169

wish that I had not left. But let's accept it that no one is indispensable.

Organisations are always bigger than individuals.

As mature professionals we simply accept such events as part of the working process and we all move on with our work. What is important is that we should keep our reputation, our integrity and our personal relations intact.

Q. 32. Do you want to ask us something?

Why is the question asked?

The interviewer is judging your self-confidence, your ability to think quickly as well as your attitude?

Answer: Most of the people will ask, either about the salary or the outcome or the result of the interview. Refrain from doing that. Instead, it is better that you ask them about the company's vision, fixture plans or something else which shows that you are concerned about your long-term future in the company. For this, you need to have studied about the company. For example, you could say that the finance minister's recent budget speech has spoken about giving a rebate to the cosmetic industry; do you think that it is going to benefit your organisation? Or you could ask, almost every big group is opening overseas offices, has your company also done that?

Questions to test your creativity and ability to think out of the box and under stress.

There are hundreds of questions that interviewers have designed. Here is a sample of such questions:

Q. 33. If you are crossing a narrow bridge and suddenly you see a train coming, you don't have the time to go back and you can't swim, what will you do?

Some other similar questions can be as follows:

Why are manholes round and not square? If there is a fire and you can save only one person, will it be your wife, your mother or your sister? What are the five uses you can put a tie to? Why is the question asked?

Managers have certainly been creative in thinking up such innovative questions. There are many more of them and your interviewer might be having some new ones in his armour. There can't be any definite answers to such questions. The basic thing is that you have to remain cool, think unconventionally and stick to a stand that you take for whatever reason. Since no answer is right or wrong, you can speak whatever you think is the right answer. You must not appear to be weak in your convictions.

Some Ready To Use Checklists

> *Matching the basic style and pace of the interviewer * Offer your full hand and not just a few fingers for a handshake * Play the interview in your mind before * Mock interviews can be a great help * Discuss with someone why you feel this is the right job * Questions related to your subject * Maintain eye contact * Most of the interviewers appreciate examples and success stories * Turning failure into success * Relax before the interview * Day dream * Practice deep breathing * Warm your face*

Carrying Your Documents And Testimonials

- The interview letter
- Photocopies of all your qualification certificates
- A copy of your CV
- The documents should be in good shape
- You must know which document is kept where so that you can retrieve it immediately without making a mess

- You must maintain a neat folder in which all your testimonials must be kept in an orderly way
- Experience certificates or other references must be kept chronologically
- Proof of age
- Visiting card of your present designation
- Are your shoes polished properly?
- Are your clothes clean and ironed properly?
- Do you have matching tie and/or socks?
- Will you look formal, yet simple in your dress?

Points To Ponder

Style of Interviewer

Matching the basic style and pace of the interviewer is very important.

If the interviewer talks rapidly or in a loud voice you talk in a very low volume or speed, he will not be comfortable with you. Remember the interviewer is the person with whom you will be working, if selected. Naturally, he will prefer a person he feels comfortable with. Similarly, if the interviewer is talking in a low volume or pace, you can not afford to talk to him in a very high volume or pace. You must try to match the interviewer's pitch and pace as far as possible. This will make the interviewer feel comfortable with you.

Some people, including interviewers, are more assertive and know clearly what they want. Such people look forward to straight, short and to the point answers. At the same time, some of the interviewers may be less sure. Such persons are usually more concerned with the politeness and manners of the candidate.

So be on the look out for which style the interviewer belongs to and ensure that you modify your communication to match his style.

Shaking The Hand Of The Interviewer

In junior level positions we should not normally offer our hand. Instead, we must wait for the interviewer to take the initiative. Some of the managers are very particular about their hygiene and may not like to shake hands with everyone. If the interviewer is interviewing some 25 candidates that day he may not like to shake everyone's hand. Therefore, it is always better to wait for the interviewer to start the process.

In case the interviewer does offer his hand for a handshake, you must offer your full hand and not just a few fingers. Your grip must be firm and the hand should be held steady for a while before letting go. When you meet friends normally, you shake the hand many times but in this case, just giving it one shake, and holding it for a short while will be appropriate. In case the interviewer is a lady your grip must be soft but the hand should be firm.

Extend a full hand firmly. A person who extends only a small part of his hand indicates a lack of trust, a certain fear. While a person who gives his full hand for a handshake shows a person who trusts and can be trusted. A firm handshake indicates that the person is confident and open to new ideas. A person who shakes your hand vigorously may be exceptionally sentimental and given to mood swings.

Play The Interview In Your Mind Before The Actual Interview

Self-suggestion is absolutely essential whenever you are going through something as crucial as an interview. You are going to appear for an interview in front of strangers, you may be surrounded by your competing candidates. You will not get any support from any one under these circumstances.

But you can be your own support. Give yourself a pat. Remind yourself how well-prepared you are for the interview. Tell yourself that you have the right qualification as well as the other required traits. Assure yourself that you will be successful. Think through every step of the interview. Play the sequence in your mind, how you may enter, how you may talk right up to the point when the interviewer gets up, shakes your hand and congratulates you for getting the job. Play this whole situation in your mind so many times that you believe you are going to get the job. Relax with a deep breathing exercise just before your turn. If you are still nervous ask yourself, what will go wrong? What worst will happen? What will I lose if I don't gain anything?

Mock Interviews Can Be A Great Help

If it were possible one would request the interviewer to take a trial interview first and then go on to the real interview. But that is not possible in the real world. There are no retakes in real life interviews. But you can have a rehearsal with a friend, relative or teacher. You can give them a script of the most likely questions and ask them to take you through an interview. The more you practice it the more confident and less nervous you will be at the time of the actual interview. Ask your dummy interviewer to be as tough and demanding as possible. A person who is himself going through the process of interviews will be the best choice to act as an interviewer.

Discuss With Someone Why You Feel This Is The Right Job For You And You Are The Right Candidate For It

Speaking your mind to someone is definitely helpful to understand your own thoughts better and to clarify them. Throwing your ideas at someone else and letting him examine them and cross-question you, is good. It is going to help you when you are putting forth those arguments to someone else.

Similarly, when you discuss with someone why it might be good for you to join a particular job, that person may ask you questions regarding this. When you find the answers to those questions you definitely become clearer about your reasons for taking up the job.

For example, if you think that you are very fit for a sales job and you discuss the same with your brother or friend; he may argue that you don't really like meeting new people and are usually keeping to yourself then how could you be successful in selling. Now, it would be good for you to think of some counter argument to that. The fact that you are forced to apply your mind to the question and to think of an answer will be very useful when you are appearing in the real interview.

Questions Related To Your Subject

While answering questions about your habits, your strengths, etc., you can not plead that you don't know or can't say. Howsoever inaccurate or unconvincing your answer may be, you will have to attempt to reply to the question. However, when it comes to questions on your textbooks, your subjects or other facts like general knowledge you must accept it if you don't know the answer. You can gracefully say that you don't know or you have an idea but are not sure. Don't make a wild guess and show false confidence.

Maintain Eye Contact

It is often said that the eyes tell more than the lips. When you speak from the heart, you tend to make more eye contact. However, some shy people by their very nature do not maintain eye contact and as a result, send a very wrong signal to the interviewer. It is generally perceived that if you don't make good eye contact you are probably not telling the truth. Maintaining eye contact definitely adds credence to what you are saying. It also reflects a positive self-

After The Interview

confidence on the part of the candidate. Eye contact does not mean keeping your eyes focused on the eyes of the other person, it means keeping your eyes around the T area, near eyes, nose, chin and forehead of the other person.

Importance Of Quoting Examples

Most of the interviewers appreciate examples and success stories. Be ready with your stories for every trait and strength that you want to mention. Few, very few interviewers may not like you to quote long examples, be vigilant of them. One sure-shot test of whether you should continue with your stories or not are to give a small pause at one stage of the story. If the interviewer grabs the opportunity and changes the subject, you may stop and go along with him. In case he does not and instead waits for you to continue, you can go ahead and complete your story. In any case you may limit yourself to shorter and to the point success stories.

Always quote the phrase or statement that your teacher, boss, friends or parents may have used to praise you. E.g., "You work like a machine" or "How can you maintain your calm in such a situation?" etc.

Turning Failure Into Success

We must do our best always but even then we should be ready to face the worst. It would be too philosophical and impractical to say do not become sad, do not worry. Some sadness is bound to take over you but don't allow this sadness to remain with you for long. Analyze the situation now with a cool mind and look at the options you have.

Learn from your failures. We must certainly be able to see what we could have done better. We must learn something from the persons who got success. A very successful sales manager told me his story. He said, "I did my schooling in a small town near Kanpur and after graduating from Kanpur University I decided to go to Delhi to attend a walk-in interview. I vividly remember the Eureka Forbes office on Asaf Ali Road, New Delhi where I went for the first interview of my life. I was dressed very simply, carrying my biodata in a cotton bag. When I entered the large room it was full of beautifully dressed people wearing ties and neatly ironed clothes. Their resumes and certificates in neat and elegant files or folders. I could not muster the courage to sit in the room and returned from the door itself. I was a thin skinny lad of 21 years at that time. After coming out of the building, I stopped to drink some water and then sat down in a park nearby. Mother had packed some *chapatis* for me as I had left my home early in the morning. I had my lunch and fell asleep in the park. When I woke up, I had this sudden feeling that I should not go back empty handed. I must gain something from this experience. So I stood near the entry to the venue of the interview. I watched the candidates leave one by one. I noticed the kind of files they were holding, the way they walked and spoke and the way they were dressed. I talked to some of them; some were indifferent but many were very understanding. That was the learning I took home with me. Gradually and surely I changed and soon I was a sales representative in a multi-national company and I never looked back."

Life's battles do not always go to the stronger and faster man. But sooner or later, the man who wins is the man who thinks he can.

Relax Before The Interview

Do you feel stressed just before an interview? Well, if you do, don't worry because you are not alone. Almost everybody including most interviewers go through some stress. Some amount of stress may in fact be desirable also. A moderate controllable level of stress may bring the best out of you and will make you put in a little extra effort. It is only when this stress goes beyond a point that it becomes undesirable or dysfunctional. What does stress do to you? Stress makes our heart beat faster, makes us sweat more, and makes our mouth dry. Some people feel nauseous also. The first common effect of excessive stress is that we are unable to think to our capacity, which can have a negative impact on our performance.

The first important thing that you need to do to tackle stress is to prepare well. At the time of the interview, you must remind yourself how hard you have prepared before the interview. You must remind yourself that most people do not prepare very well and you happen to be definitely better prepared than others.

In addition, to a good self-talk you can use the following techniques to relax just before the interview:

Day Dreaming

You can day dream and take yourself to the best garden of your city or to the hill station you like most or you could imagine sitting with an old friend and talking about old things. This conscious and deliberate day dreaming can blow away your tension. Close your eyes, sit comfortably on your chair and take your thoughts through the complete process of what you are imagining. For example, let us suppose that you want to go to your favourite hill station. Now you take your thoughts to the moment when you sit down with your family to decide and to work out the details. In your mind, think about the mode of transport you decide to take, the hotel you will stay in and people who will go along with you. After this, you go through the complete process of enjoying the holiday – day dream about the minute details.

Deep Breathing

This is one of the best relaxation exercises that you can do while waiting your turn for the interview. Just close your eyes, sit erect on your chair keeping your spine straight. Take a deep breath, hold it for a little while and then exhale slowly. Keep all your attention on observing what happens to your stomach and chest while inhaling and exhaling. Your stomach must rise when you inhale and it must fall when you exhale. The movement in the chest should be very little. Repeat deep breathing five to ten times and you will feel more relaxed.

Warm Your Face

Rub your palms hard against each other; a little heat will be generated. Now take both your palms and make the same motion that one makes while washing ones face. Feel the warmth of your hands transfer to your face and flow through the whole mind and body.

EPILOGUE

Once the interview is over, play it again in your mind. Think and note down as to where you did well and where you could have done better. This analysis can be done by you only and will be done best within a few minutes after the interview is over.

Next, you must write to the interviewer thanking him for the interview. In case the interviewer has promised to call you up by a particular date but does not do so, you can give him a ring and speak to him. Even if the interviewer had said it casually, that he would be calling you up, it does give you a right to expect his call. Many times the selected candidate does not join and the next waiting list candidate is being considered. Suppose that, meanwhile your call comes through and even if you are third on the waiting list there are great chances that you could be considered.

By calling and writing after the interview, you will be showing how serious you are about the job. You also show yourself as a person who likes to take his work to its logical conclusion. It will also impress that you don't shirk work but instead like to do extra work beyond the expected level.

Finally, before we close let us have some more thoughts on 'Winning the Race – The Game of Interview'.

1. Always project yourself as a person who is willing to accept and adopt change. A person who is open to new ideas and ways of doing things is better accepted.
2. If you know computers, you must express clearly how this knowledge is going to help you do a better job, if selected. The point is that while computer knowledge is necessary, it is useful only if it is in relevant areas. That relevance you must state clearly to the interviewer.

3. Repeatedly show your orientation (bent of mind) towards profits. You must show that you know how important it is to keep the cost of operation low and the revenue high.
4. Know your priorities and if you are in a position to do so, do bargain for your benefits but only after you have been offered the job. You certainly need to negotiate and get the best of benefits possible. However, first you must clarify the role you would be playing, the support you would be getting in accomplishing your goals, the clarity of the goals and then should come the money part. Always have a long-term perspective and think of how you can be successful in the assignment that you are being given.
5. Think about the profile of the company's customers, executives, workers, competitors, etc. Think of the business they are into. This will help you understand the needs of the organisation interviewing you, more clearly.
6. You must show more concern for the kind of work you will be doing rather than the designation you will be appointed for and the size of the cabin you will be using.
7. Irrespective of the department for which you are being interviewed for, you must show concern for customer service. Genuine interest in making the customer's happy is the need of the hour for every organisation.
8. You must firmly believe and let known your belief that giving is more important than receiving; and that if you do your job well and give results to the organisation, the organisation is going to take good care of you.

■ ■ ■